CLASH MAGAZINE

ISSUE #1

Edited by
LEZA CANTORAL & CHRISTOPH PAUL

CONTENTS

INTRODUCTION

A year ago I made a Zine & it was rad, but Zines take freaking forever to make & even though they are gorgeous & I love them, it just was not practical. Some of the poems from that Zine made it into this magazine & that makes me so happy. Just because this is printed by a machine does not mean it does not have the heart of those handmade Zines I stayed up all night making, getting bleary-eyed & manic, my hands covered in glue & paper-cuts. Whether you are reading this on printed paper or digitally, know that the words are real.

Leza Cantoral

We thought managing a website would be fun, we thought running a press would be even more fun. We were right, but damn, it is not easy. So many things can go wrong and you can only learn by doing. It's not that different from the bands I've played in, sometimes the shows are great, sometimes we'll bomb. Sometimes books sell and sometimes they don't. What makes it worth it? It's the simple, the writers themselves. Their words are gifts that we get package up and put out in the world. It makes me feel like a punk rock Santa Claus bringing these stories to you.

Christoph Paul

NON-FICTION

LIST OF THINGS THAT DON'T MAKE YOU A WRITER: GABINO IGLESIAS

1. Owning a laptop.
2. Going to a coffee shop.
3. Owning a cat.
4. Putting the word author in your Twitter bio.
5. Drinking/talking about/enjoying coffee.
6. Living next to a university.
7. Hanging out with writers.
8. Telling people you're working on something.
9. Putting on a "funny" literary shirt.
10. Naming your pets after characters in famous novels.
11. Reading Rick Moody or pretending to have read and/or enjoyed David Foster Wallace and Thomas Pynchon.
12. Having a Goodreads account.
13. Listening to obscure bands that like to use more than twenty words per song.
14. Watching a lot of art films.
15. Complaining about the state of publishing.
16. Going to AWP.
17. Saying authors are your heroes.
18. Hating James Patterson.
19. Hating YA.
20. Talking about writing on Facebook.
21. Sharing fake word counts.
22. Being unemployed.
23. Lounging.

24. Being a fucking beer snob.
25. Wearing glasses.
26. Correcting your friends' grammar.
27. Describing yourself as an author/writer/wordsmith.
28. Living in an artsy (aka gentrified) part of town.
29. Applying to low residency MFAs.
30. Having ideas.
31. Thinking you have what it takes to write a novel.
32. Reading more than ten books per year.
33. Skimming through literary blogs.
34. Claiming no one understands you.
35. Buying a typewriter.

SOMEONE ELSE'S BIG BREAK: DANGER SLATER

I'm a security guard. This is my day job.

Believe it or not, writing weirdo Bizarro horror books doesn't *quite* pay the bills. Shocking, I know.

I always assumed I'd end up rich and famous someday. It seemed inevitable. I'm smart(-ish) and ambitious(-ish) and have a lot of (arguably) good(-ish) talents. I always thought, with all these innate advantages at my disposal, it would only be a matter of time before EVERYONE else noticed how AMAZING I was too.

I was like: charter me a jet and fly me to a resort in the Maldives and serve me up a big ol' bowl of smoked caviar for breakfast, or whatever the fuck it is rich people eat for breakfast.

Why would I waste my time TRYING when I was JUST THAT DAMN GOOD?

Turns out, I'm poor. Like no-health-insurance-or-gas-in-my-car-poor. I live in a small apartment with my girlfriend and her kids. We can't even afford HBO. People are always going on and on about "last night's *Game of Thrones*" and I never have any idea what they're talking about. Didn't some dude bang his sister or something? See, I don't even know!

So earlier this summer, I was working backstage a three-day blue-grass music festival. I was in charge of checking wristbands; making sure only the "right" people got through to the greenroom area and everyone else kept on moseying along. It was an easy gig, all things considered. I didn't have to do all that much. But these were LONG days. BORING days. And I had several of them in a row.

So about 45 hours into my 60 hour weekend, this guy came up to me. A young dude. Maybe in his mid-20s. He looked like approximately 75% of the people I've met since I moved to Portland last year – lopsided man bun on the top of his head, wide bushy beard like an overgrown hedge, pants as tight as lizard skin. He was the kind of person that would normally fade into the walls. Generic. Forgettable. Another dude in a sea of dudes.

He slowly stepped up to me.

"Hey man, I'm in a band," he said.

"That's great," I laconically replied, completely disinterested because EVERYONE at this entire festival was in some kind of band.

"We were playing an acoustic set on the side of the trail to the main stage earlier this morning…"

"Oh right, I saw that when I was heading down here," I said. "You had your CDs out for sale and everything."

"Those were demos, actually," he told me. "We couldn't get on the bill for the festival, so we figured we'd just come out and play anyway. Fuck it, right? What's the worst that could happen? They make us stop?"

"Fair enough," I said.

"Hey, so I was wonderin', do you think I can maybe get backstage?" he said, eyebrows arched up expectantly, like a kid asking for extra dessert.

This was it. My time to shine. I was gonna lay a big fat GET THE FUCK OUTTA HERE on this guy. This was why they hired me.

"Well, you see, that's the problem," I said. "The reason I'm standing here to make sure that only people with a black wristband get backstage. And your wristband, unfortunately, is light blue, and light blue means general admission. So, as I'm sure you already knew, that's a no-go, buddy."

"Right, I know that's," he said. "But there's a dude hanging out back there right now who hosts this radio show… I was hoping to get a word with him. Chat him up. Maybe slip him one of the demos. I don't know, man."

"Unfortunately, I want to get paid at the end of this weekend, so I gotta do what they asked me to do."

"C'mon, man, there's gotta be something you can do for me?" he said.

"Alright, I'll tell you what…you can stand here, right OUTSIDE the backstage area, and when I see the radio dude you're looking for, I'll give you a little nod and you can chat him up on his way back to his camp."

The guy in the band seemed okay with this. He had little recourse. I wasn't about to let him backstage. Like I said, he had the wrong wristband. I was the wristband police. I was the fucking Governor of Wristband Island.

For two hours he stood there, stretching his neck up, trying to see over my shoulder towards the greenroom, trying to spot the elusive DJ getting drunk at the open bar, back there with all the headlining acts.

And I watched him. I spent two hours watching him. I spent two hours watching him and thought: There's a reason there are no rock star novelists. Music is easy. Music breathes. A song will float by on the breeze as light as the air itself. It will bounce around inside your head and find its way into your limbs and live in your bones. And that's a beautiful thing. But reading...shit, you have to give up part of your life in order to let a book inside you. Reading is sacrifice. It takes time to consume, and even more time to settle. Trying to get someone to read a book (trying to get someone to read one of MY books) is like asking them if they want to enter a committed relationship. As such, us writers have to sneak in slowly. Quietly. The seeds we sow we rarely see harvested. When the person on stage finishes playing a song, the crowd erupts into cheers and applause. When someone finishes reading a books, they close the cover, and put on a shelf.

At times being a writer feels like a curse. Like a burden I'm always dragging around behind me. It feels a lot less like what-I-do and a lot more like who-I-am.

And then there was this guy in front of me. Tenaciously standing there. Audaciously waiting. Doing what he could, doing ANYTHING he could, to find an in, even though there was a wall in his way. I WAS HIS WALL.

And then I thought: Life is fucking hard enough, ya know? If we have nothing (and we often have nothing) there's always that ONE THING we cling to. You know that thing. I know you do. It's that blind, vague, pointless hope. That stupid little light inside, that for whatever reason, doesn't let us quit. Goddamn, sometimes it goes dim. Sometimes it feels like it goes out completely. And then there it is again. It's the foolish notion that someday we will receive our reward; that caviar breakfasts are just on the other side of that horizon.

And that's it, right there. Being an artist in a nutshell. More than being an artist. Being a goddamn human being. It doesn't matter if you're smart(-ish) and ambitious(-ish) and have a lot of (arguably) good(-ish) talents. This shit is HARD. Every day, it's HARD. And if you want to do something important with your life, you got to hold onto that hope, as stupid as that may be.

"Hey listen," I eventually said to him, leaning in close and putting my arm around his shoulder, my voice going low in his ear, barely above a whisper. "Around the other side of the mainstage here, if you come up through the woods, I saw a hole in the fence that looked just big enough for a person to squeeze through. Now I'm not telling you to go through this hole. I would NEVER tell you to do that. In fact, were I to notice such a hole, I should probably tell one of the event organizers so that they send someone over there to close it up. But as it were, since I have to stand here and check wristbands and there doesn't seem to be any of the event organizers around, if someone were to come up through the breach in the fence, and I happened NOT to see it go down, well then...there's really not too much I can do about that, is there?"

The guy's face went wide. A sloppy smile, pinching up around the corner of his eyes. Then he walked away.

I didn't see him for the rest of the night.

But the next morning, I bumped into him at his camp. He was eating breakfast with the rest of his band. Nothing fancy. Just a regular breakfast. Orange juice and granola bars. I walked over towards him to say hi.

"So how'd your evening go?" I asked.

He threw his arms around me and gave me a giant hug, picking me up and dropping me back down in one jovial motion. "Dude!" he exclaimed. "It was incredible! I got to talk to that DJ guy and we're going to be performing LIVE on the radio tomorrow! This could be it! Thank you so much!"

I waved his off his gratitude with a dismissive hand. "Don't thank me," I said to the guy. "I didn't 'let you in' back there. YOU found the hole."

I don't really know what the point of this story is. Did I do a good deed? Yeah, maybe. Maybe I'm owed one. Maybe one day karma will smile upon me too.

Or maybe I'm just shitty at my job.

THAT SCRAP BOOK: ANONYMOUS

My mother has a scrap book that she keeps on the coffee table. There are pictures of my sisters and I with our cousins, all of our school photos, napkins and match books and coasters from retirement parties and graduations and weddings. In this scrap book is full of things I don't want to remember, things I'm not proud of, mementos of an unmemorable rural life. I have spent that life being told that I am better than African Americans, Latinos, Jews, and homosexuals. Sometimes I was told violently. Sometimes I was told earnestly. Whatever the mode of delivery, the refrain was the same: blacks could not be trusted, Puerto Ricans wanted to rape me, and that lesbians would try to convert me.

The first picture we see is six-year-old me standing in the dining room of our house, the pink of my sweatshirt clashing with the green window frame. We just moved in. My father's voice booms out over the kitchen, not aggressive but not *not* aggressive. In this memory, I'm not sure if he's in this picture. If he is, maybe he's cut out of frame just slightly, but I know I'm standing by the window because the window plays a big part in this. My mother, I'm pretty sure, is sitting at the table.

"If you ever bring a black man home, I'm throwing you through that window." My mother nods furiously in agreement.

I don't understand the sexual context, the over sexualization of the statement, or even how or why I would bring a black man home. At six years old, I am more concerned with learning to tie my shoes than I am about interracial marriage. For a month, every day after school I am vigilant about checking my backpack for interloping black men. For a few weeks I have nightmares about being thrown through the window. I suspect now my father's outburst must have had something to do with one of my many older cousins dating a mulatto boy, or as my father calls him to his face later that summer, a "mutt". It's 1991.

Years later, my parents inevitable divorce takes place, I ask my mother about that statement and its repetition over the years and why she sided with my father. Her response?

"He was my husband. I had to agree with him."

My mother has a Southern Belle's fear of black men which is ironic since she grew up in a rural town just outside of Poughkeepsie and raised us in the same area. As my sisters and I grow older and begin to date, she warns us about the lascivious sexual appetites of black men and their goal to "ruin" white girls. She cites my cousin and her ex-boyfriend, the mutt, for reference. Today my cousin is a successful web developer and married to a detective. They have four beautiful kids. Racism doesn't always require accurately citing your sources.

This next photo is from 1993 and I'm eight years old at a school Christmas sing along. I trip coming off the choral risers because the cuff of my jeans get caught on the corner. The music teacher catches me with a smile and a pat. The bleachers are filled with parents ready to take their sugared up kids home for Christmas break. My father meets me, red in the face, and my mother tugs on his sleeve to prevent a scene. At this point I'm good at gauging shit storms and my mood plummets. I am in trouble. I don't know for what, but the why of things has stopped mattering. We get to the car in silence. It is not until we are almost home when my father turns around.

"Does that jigaboo push you around a lot?" At eight, I find a strange pride in knowing a racial or derogatory term for almost every letter of the alphabet. I dawned on me that he assumed the black girl behind me, I think her name might have been Jennifer or Jessie, pushed me off the choral risers. I could say no, and he wouldn't believe me. I could say yes and he'd blow up at me for not socking her in the face. I say nothing and eventually it blows over.

Go back almost a decade to 1989 and this memory is more yellowed, the edges of the photo paper rounded off. My mother and her Godmother are talking about leaving the small Methodist church they attended for almost a decade because of the new Korean minister and his weird smell. He smells so bad, according to my mother, that she can smell him all the way from the back of the church. I'm almost four and have a that annoying toddler instinct to repeat everything I hear. I say loudly in church the next Sunday that I didn't smell anything funny. My mother recounts this story through out my life as if I came up with the idea our pastor smelled funny by myself.

This next photo jumps ahead to 2004 and I'm a senior in high school. My parents have given my sisters and I a sex talk that mostly included "don't get pregnant" and a more aggressive refrain about being thrown through the dinning room window if we bring home black men. I have my own car and am friends with mostly gay guys and the nerdy girls who are madly in love with them. My purity is definitely not at stake. Band practice runs late one day and a friend asks me to give him a ride home. He's a foot shorter than I am and about 25lbs lighter. His father is the town's chief of police and he is black. His father is white. I drop him off and his African American mother waves from the porch as I wave back. I like his family, they're nice people. He's not my type though he's asked me out before. My mother finds out about both the ride home from school and that he's asked me out and takes my keys away for a month.

Jump forward two years and I'm in my sophomore year of college. There's pixelation and smudges on the paper since I haven't gotten the hang of printing pictures yet. I'm living in the dorms. My RA is black, the resident director is black, and the housing director is Latina. I have a white roommate and I'm embarrassingly relieved about this. We have a very diverse student body; a diversity that shocked me like cold water to the face at first but one that I've come to be comfortable in. I'm starting to realize that we are all human and that being afraid of people because of their appearances is something ignorant people do. After all, I no longer live with my family and I'm starting to see what healthy and unhealthy relationships look like. I'm starting to learn that sometimes the people you call family are more dangerous than some black man walking behind you in a parking lot.

My seventh grade school picture from 1997. I have stopped smiling in school photos by now. My sister is dating a blond haired, blue eyed boy with the last name Martinez. He goes to our school and wears Carhart jackets and Dickies pants, he takes the first day of hunting season off every year. He wears a John Deere hat and is the president of Future Farmers of America. My mother works with his father, but my parents are still cautious - he might be Puerto Rican. My father hates

Puerto Ricans more than he hates blacks, but only slightly more. The story he tells us is about his childhood in the verdant garden district of Vernon, New Jersey where migrant workers lived in shanties to help bring in harvests during the late 60s and 70s. One summer, my father recounts, they were "overrun" with Puerto Ricans. In his typical white rural clip, he pronounces it *Purrt-Oh Rick-in*. His beloved baby sister, my Aunt Helen, was 16 at the time and an absolute angel. She went missing one warm summer night and threw my Catholic grandparents into a panic. The men of the family searched the fields and the barns and came up empty. My aunt returned home bruised and scratched in the early morning hours and claimed she had been abducted by a group of "spics" and raped. The way my father tells the rest of this story makes a small crack in who I am. According to him, he, my grandfather, several of my great-uncles, and most of the men from the meandering clan of my father's extended family descended on the shanty town where the migrant workers lived. They burned the shanties and bungalows, rounded up men of likely age and beat them. My father always smiles when he tells this story and this time is no different. "There are bodies," he says. "There are bodies that won't ever be found." I am thirteen. My sister stops dating the Martinez boy.

This next snapshot is a bleary yellow polaroid of my father, his head ducked out of the shot last minute so his features are blurred. You can only clearly see an ear. To understand my father you need to understand failed machismo, the staggering weight a man bears when he's incredibly intelligent, more than intelligent enough to realize how thoroughly he's fucked up his own life. That's the kind of machismo that makes you wish you'd actually killed someone when you hadn't. My Aunt Helen and my grandmother recount this story for me when I'm 18. Their version is cleaner but just as malicious. Helen had been getting drunk with some boys from high school and ended up screwing one of them in a hayloft. They lost track of time and started smoking weed. She fell out of the hayloft and I guess falling ten feet onto handpicked dirt and hay jolted her into some type of sobriety and she realized how late it was. The fall from the hayloft gave her the bumps and scrapes she needed to pass off a rough night. She blamed it on an unfortunate group of teenage boys and my grandfather went berserk. According to my grandmother, he drove around until he found one abandoned bungalow and burned it. They broke some windows and my dad roughed up an unsuspecting Italian kid who had the misfortune to look Puerto Rican. Nobody was killed, but both my aunt and grandmother think the story is funny. My grandmother had helped Aunt Helen come up with the lie so my grandfather didn't kick her out.

"This is shameful. This is such a shameful time for this country," my mother says with tears in her eyes. It's 2008 and Barak Obama just won the Presidential Election. She says she's upset because he's a Democrat but I know it's because he's black. This picture is as smooth and clear as a professional portrait.

"Look. Just look at this! She has an Adam's Apple!" My father-in-law waves a magazine in my face. He's pointing to Michelle Obama. "She's really a man. Look at that square jaw and monkey brow. She's a man!" He laughs at his cleverness. "Michael Obama." It's 2012 and Barak Obama has been reelected President of the US. We hear this often.

A blurry 2009 cell phone picture of my first apartment. I've finished my first year at graduate school in a small city in New Jersey. I'm live 3 hours from home. My parent's divorce is final. My mother and sister visit me to cheer themselves up. My apartment is small and secure. There are key codes to the front door, the stairwells and the elevator. From my window I can barely make out the spires of a Mosque. A family of Muslims live across the street from me. My sister sees the mother take her children for a walk and asks, fear flashing across her face, if we should call the police.

Two days after my wedding, my husband and I are cleaning up yard and helping pack up the folding chairs as my mother talks to whoever is listening. She is talking about nonsensical things and then switches gears. "I'm glad Carrie didn't come." She's talking about my sister's best friend. I ask why, since she always like Carrie. My mother giggles, a hopeful look on her face mingled with a firm smile. She's going to say something horrible and wants me to agree with her. " She would have brought her kid. That halfbreed of hers. I'm sorry but it's just wrong to have a black man's baby." The napkin I'm holding reads June 5th, 2015.

Some pages of this album have stuck together and we must peel them apart. I used too much glue for this photo, maybe on purpose, maybe to damage it. It's one of my grandparent's 50th wedding anniversaries or maybe it's someone's retirement party. I don't know. I'm making the rounds with my father, a huge smile on my face. He's parading me around table to table and stopping conversations. "Listen to this joke my kid tells." I've told this joke about five times and I feel prouder every time. A lot of my uncles are drunk and are giving me quarters or dollar bills for telling this joke. The joke goes like this:

A white man walks into a bar and sees three blacks sitting at the counter. He bets them that he's stronger than they are. They take the bet and they go up the roof to settle it. The white man bets the first black man that he can't jump off the roof of the bar and bounce. The man takes the bet and jumps. He dies. The second black man gets upset but the white guy holds him back and say *"hey, watch me"*. The white man proceeds to jump off the roof, bounce lightly off the pavement, and land without a scratch back on the roof. Emboldened, the next black man tries it and dies. The cycle repeats again with the third black man. A man inside the bar asks the owner what all the commotion is and the owner replies "oh, that's just Superman fucking with a bunch of Niggers." I am almost nine. I am wearing a blue dress.

This picture is a speckled and too-orange employee ID. An obese white man sits across from me. He has a noose tattooed on his forearm and swastikas on the knuckles of his right hand. He has needle tacks pocking the ink of the tattoos like bloody potholes. I'm helping him fill out a public assistance application that will allow him to receive safe housing, food stamps, and addiction services as well as enroll him in Medicaid. The Affordable Care Act has been in effect for five years. He is a felon. He injected his 8 months pregnant girlfriend with a lethal dose of heroin because he wanted her to party with him again like she did before she got pregnant. She lost the baby and almost died. I finish the application and tell him I don't see any reason why he should be denied assistance. He gives me a level look. "Oh, it'll be denied. Prob'ly because of some knocked up Mexican whore welfare rat. That's why."

It is summer and my hand is mostly covering the lens in this picture; you can see my bare feet and that I'm in that awkward stage of preadolescence where I need to be reminded to comb my hair and then defiantly don't. I'm eleven and not old enough to stay home alone yet according to my father. I accompany him to a big building with marble columns. He files a bunch of paperwork and the lady behind the counter says she's sorry for our circumstances and gives me a lollipop. I'm not sure what's so wrong with our circumstances, but hey. Free lollipop. We drive forty-five minutes with the windows down and the greens and golds of the Hudson Valley splatter past. We get to another big building. My father pulls a back brace out of the back seat and wiggles it up over his beer belly. "Don't say anything about the other lady to this lady, understand?" I nod because I don't really care. I'm in the middle of a Goosebumps book and all I care about is what happens to the garden gnomes. My father files papers and I get another lollipop and more sympathy. A black man holds the door for us as we leave and my father sneers at him. "That man has never worked a day in his life, I guarantee it." Later on I will realize that my father was fraudulently cross filing unemployment and disability claims in multiple counties.

Filter free and with stunning clarity, this is a picture of a bright blue ocean. My husband and I don't visit our relatives anymore, or at least we try not to. When we do we keep the visits short and direct the conversation as strongly as we can toward the weather (a hoax) our respective jobs or degrees (a waste). We scrape and save enough for small island honeymoon almost two years after our wedding. My father-in-law tells us not to go, that it's dangerous for white people to leave American soil right now. There is no evidence of this that isn't produced from Breitbartesque chatrooms.

This is a picture torn out of a magazine with a recipe on one side and an article for laser hair removal on the other. My grandmother saves articles she thinks we're interested in. Towards the end, she gives us jaggedly torn shreds that cut the article in half or made no sense, or was a pull out add for men's erectile dysfunction meds. I'm home from college for a long weekend. My sister and I take our grandmother out to lunch. Her dementia is getting worse and we shouldn't have let her pick the restaurant. She thinks we're at a diner she frequented back in the 90s. Same location, but now it's an Applebees. From the parking lot I can see the MTA station and the commuters hustling back and forth, trying to keep warm on the platform. A group of young black men come in and are seated across from us. My grandmother locks up in fear. She won't finish her lunch. My sister and I sit there, praying she doesn't say anything.

These next two are audio clips. I talk to my mother about Treyvon Martin. She says it's a shame he's dead but it was his own fault. "They shouldn't wear hoodies," she says. "Or keep their hands in their pockets." She's turning sixty soon.

"They recommended that Tiffany be removed from the school." My mother is telling me about my cousin's daughter, who was in an altercation on her first day of first grade.

"What did she do?"

My mother laughs. "She said was she didn't want to sit next to a dirty Mexican and then pushed the little girl out of the seat next to her." The other little girl hit her head on the corner of the desk when she fell and needed stitches. This is left out of the story for me to find out later.

This last picture is dark. It is a dark alley from my apartment building to the parking garage. There is a small courtyard where the parking garage meets the building. Anemic trees stretch for light that hardly filters down between the two concrete walls, studded with exit doors and air conditioners. A young black man is leaning against the tree. I check my purse and realize I don't have my phone or my mace. The young man is in a button down shirt and slacks. He's smoking a cigarette and looking at his phone. I stop, he looks at me and my heart drops to my feet. I can't get my keys out fast enough or run back into my building because that exit is a dead bolt that takes forever to open. He sees the panic on my face and sighs.

"I'm not going to hurt you, you know. I'm just on my break." He says this like it's for the fifth time tonight. I say nothing and shuffle past. The closer I get, I realize he's probably in his teens. I'm 24.

The things I'm showing you are not things I'm proud of. It is a scrapbook of what I can't ignore anymore. They are stories that hurt me to tell because I still love some of these people, even though I know they're toxic. What strikes me the most, weights the heaviest, is my silence. The times I didn't say anything, the times I didn't stand up. My silence is probably my biggest privilege and was my only armor; if I hide and say nothing I will not be the target. The ability to shrug it off and say it isn't my problem is woven around the cracks in the stone and mortar foundation of who I am.

We talk about racism as if it's a past relic. As if it is something that has been taken out of context or as if it's a conspiracy created keep poor white people down. This fall I watched the lid come off the can of all the worms I was fed during my childhood and I worry about my cousins' children, I worry about my nieces and nephews. Racism is born of toxicity and anger and a need to destroy. It consumes people so much that they feel the need to tell their six year old that they'll throw them through the window, and then years later brag about killing a man. Racism is human uranium and racists boil and burn until they become a tiny Chernobyl and that toxicity leaks out. They have to take it out on someone, that bullying, just like it was taken out on them. Racism, for all it's ugliness and darkness, has turned on a light for me. Toxic people in my life have always exposed their toxicity by being racist. It's subtle, a wink-wink-nudge-nudge glance or comment. It's an assumed inclusion until told otherwise, its extreme offense at being called a racist while not being upset or outraged about real racial injustice.

I don't know happened to my father to make him create a fantasy in which he kills a bunch of teenage migrants, but I can guess. My mother's family makes jokes about my grandfather's right hook, and about the fact that as a cop he called his night shifts "coon hunting." Racism, like abuse, is systemic. It's learned. And it won't stop unless we stop - unless we question our parents, our beliefs. It will not end unless we stop it.

SANTA MUERTE: THE ALTAR BECOMES MY INJECTION SITE: MONIQUE QUINTANA

PICTURES BY DR. PATRICK FONTES

Hands out, she doesn't judge or balance scales. She listens and does what I ask her to do, not what she thinks is best for me. For this, I know to not take her lightly. But she is positive about death. She lets me know that my own death is inevitable and is coming soon.

She is an outlawed saint.

She's skeletal and not recognized by the Catholic Church. I never wanted to be Catholic, but I find solace in ritual. If I could, I'd probably joint the Iglesia Santa Católica Apostólica Tradicional Mex-USA because they recognize Muerte and our more attuned to my leftist politics. To them, she is sacred and not to be shamed.

She doesn't heed specific directions, because death is fluid and so, she is everywhere.

Altars to Muerte map the border like stars. Wives and children and drug lords and sex workers speak to her. And sometimes there are stars on the cloak that covers her head. Make an altar only for her. Take a textile and cover the base. My cover is thick red ribbon with gold glitter bits, wrapped around and around on a shelf, hooked in the wall of my bedroom. Her image should be there. My death's face is on $1.99 candle from a box grocery store, a pool of thick black wax in a long skinny glass, like a needle. The altar becomes my injection site.

I burn sticks and cones and candles to her. There is petition in fire and smoke. I adore it when things smell like death. Not the actual dead body, but the things that are set on fire because the body is dead. Like beads of copal on a tiny disk of charcoal, smoke black like a saucer dressed in cheap meteor and light.

There is the tequila shot of love because agave burns and is a container of memories. A plant and a tool plowed by my ancestors. Small and dark and slanted eyed like me. To remind me of times I make contact with my Mexicaness, and I get burned in the throat.

A wand of black tourmaline. For protection from those that would cause me harm. For the demons I can't see yet. The absence of color. The neutralizer. My cloak and my shoes and my dress and my lipstick.

Fresh flowers cut from my garden. Flowers hung and dried of its' corpse and song. No pomp or circumstance is necessary. Plastic roses from carnivals lit up and battery blue. They're all divine and garden, crushed up in her cup.

ANGRY OLD MEN: JUSTIN GRIMBOL

I work as a Home Health Aid. I visit old people in their homes and help them with daily tasks, like cooking and cleaning and bathing. This can be awkward, because as soon as the clients and their family see me and how sloppy I look, they know I am not any good at any of these life skills. I look like a stray dog. Not a professional. I'm surprised people don't complain.

The agency I work for gives me the clients that are considered difficult. They are usually men with bad tempers. They yell and curse too much. Some people respond to anger and cursing like its pornography. I'm very suspicious of people who are like this. I find these old men endearing. I love their easy anger. And their cursing.

Recently the agency sent me to a guy living in Burtonsville, VT. This man had a real knack for cursing. He told me he was originally, which meant he was not a Vermonter. I am also from Long Island. I had migrated to Vermont for college and got attached to all the syrupy hippy women, the muddy roads, and the diners.

"You ever miss Long Island?" I asked.

"Fuck no."

"Too crowded right?"

"I don't like that kind bull shit."

"You like Vermont?"

He waved his middle finger around and mumbled something that involved a lot of curse words.

"Why did you move here?"

"A fucking woman," he said.

Then he laughed.

"So what do you need help with today?" I asked.

"I don't fucking know."

"You got any laundry?"

"Fuck laundry," he said. "I don't care about that shit."

I asked him if he wanted me to make him something for lunch.

"Fuck no," he said.

He pulled out a large hunting knife and cut open a box of cookies and ate a few.

I sat down and relaxed. His apartment was barren. There was nothing on the walls. Just a large window.

"You got a nice view here," I said. "Look at all those fucking trees out there and that creek. It's beautiful."

"It is," he said. "It's very good."

He offered me a cookie. I told him I was on a diet.

After some light cleaning, I headed home. It was snowing so I had to drive slowly.

I kept thinking about his cookies and how badly I wanted to dip those cookies in coffee and eat them until I grew stretch marks.

My grandma used to have cookies like that. She kept them in a round tin. I miss my grandmother terribly, even though she hated cursing. She especially hated curse words that referred to sex. She also hated cold weather. And she hated money. "The rich keep getting richer," she would say. "And the poor keep getting poorer." I'm glad she did not live to see a Trump presidency. The perfect storm of money, greed, and foul language I've ever seen.

Towards the end of her life, my grandmother had become bitter and worn down from being blind, living in federal housing, and having her husband die so slowly and so sloppily.

"You can't tell me this life is blessed," she'd say. She would bitch about things and drink Miller High Life with me. She wasn't a drinker. But during my visits, she would allow herself a few beers. Sometimes she'd even curse and laugh. When I was little, she was a lot of fun. She'd give me gum drops and twizzlers and soda. Sometimes she'd get really goofy and start singing to me in Danish. And I would dance naked and giggling like I was being tickled by hundreds of guppy-sized ghosts.

As I drove through the messy Vermont roads, I thought about my grandmother and I missed her and I wondered why I cursed in front of her so much. I felt bad about being so bratty and rude.

Eventually I got home. My driveway was too steep and slippery so I parked at the bottom and had to walk up to my cabin. I was surprised to see that way my wife and dog were outside. She was sitting in a rocking chair we had left out all winter.

"Hey baby," she said. "Can you believe this weather? When is spring going to get here?"

"I know," I said. "It's lousy."

"No, it's not actually that bad. I mean it's snowing like a mother-fucker. But it's not that bad."

WATCH ME TWEET ABOUT BEING HUMAN GARBAGE & CHILL? BRIAN ALAN ELLIS

Welcome to social media, where a thing you put your heart and soul into gets significantly less likes than that random picture of ALF you posted, because social media runs on sad desperation, misguided attempts at personal substantiation, and cats, and whenever I comment on someone's post and they don't acknowledge/engage me by liking my comment and/or commenting back I just assume they either

a) hate me, b) have their lives together, or c) are too old to fully understand how social media actually works,

so consider this a shout-out to the people who wish that someone would dump cold water on the people who constantly post videos of themselves performing shitty folk songs, and let's discover the emoticon for when we feel nothing but wish to express that we feel nothing, and let's start the year exactly how we started and ended the previous year—by shamelessly promoting our "content" while knowing that those articles about how to properly use social media platforms are pointless because all you really need is low self-worth and a weakness for empty validation, which is cake, so let's wish crippling depression on those who "check-in" to artisanal restaurants/post things like "Hey [insert place], I'm gonna be in you soon!"

and let's school those who invite us to like their "There's Hope for the Human Race Walkathon" Facebook pages, and let's all scream into a virtual abyss, and let's take our Tumblr accounts out behind the wood-shed and shoot the fuck out of them with paintball guns, and let's *Fahrenheit 451* Goodreads, and let's resuscitate Ello and Friendster but leave Myspace and LiveJournal in the past, and let's open an Instagram account where pictures are posted of people passed out in their locked, exhaust-fumed cars while wearing the latest seasonal fashions, and let's block everyone who succumbs to political hyperbole, and let's clasp our hands together and thank our dear Lord for all the likes and retweets we've received, and when my Kickstarter launches I'll sweeten the deal by letting you help me shamefully binge-eat one of those frozen chocolate cream pies they recommend you thaw before serving but whatevz, so go ahead and laugh at my miserable outbursts; it's fine —just know that I'm here for you—but don't call or text me; I prefer to be tagged—

and how can Facebook expect me to share my Facebook memories when I can't even handle my Facebook realities?—and why have kids when you can have multiple social media accounts that are just as disappointing/draining/time-consuming?—and today on Twitter Wars it's The Entrepreneurs vs. The Bootleg Rappers vs. The Millennial Poets vs. The Feminist Yoga Spiritualists vs. The Armchair Politicians vs. The Bitter Comedians, and today on Facebook Wars it's the people who post bullshit questions vs. the people who smugly think, "I got this," then immediately reply with a bullshit answer,

and last night I dreamed I tweeted "You're a nihilist? Cool! What do you nihil?" and then my laptop exploded in the dream and I awoke in a panic but mainly because I'd just had a nightmare involving social media, which is way too Thom Yorke for my liking, but luckily my Tinder profile says, "I don't vote, or eat veggies; I avoid the outdoors/spend way too much time online; I don't own a car; I still use a flip phone; my cat is dope; date me," and luckily my Craigslist missed connection says, "You were the creepy drunk dude from last night who growled and then completely ate shit while trying to jump a fence as my friend and I bicycled past. Thought you were a dog, dude. Scary as fuck. Hella impressed by your quick recovery, though. Mad skills,"

and I once fantasized about having a panic attack while being interviewed via Skype and the person interviewing me having to call 911 from another state and then Skype asking me to add a "mood message" and it was like, do they even want to go there?—and a Checkers burger will always be more satisfying than a verified Twitter account check mark, and the cause of our collective deaths will involve an overuse of hashtags—#FF: @fuckyou, @666, @killyourself, @plzdie, @HolyShit-ThisIsStupid—and social media as a whole has made us into cartoon characters of our own neuroses, so [insert Porky Pig voice] that's all, folks!

DC PORN STORE BOOK CLUB: ANNA KARENINA: CHRISTOPH PAUL

Halfway through working on my MFA in creative writing, I was writing my novel/thesis literary novel titled Prophet. I reread the classics for inspiration and for my thesis while simultaneously managing a North East DC porn store during the day. When it was slow, many of the regulars (a couple African-American men in their early fifties) would come in and ask me about the books I was reading. Through these encounters I started the unofficial book club for the DC Perverts/Literary Curious. Here is a recollection of our meeting when we reviewed the merits of the Russian literary classic Anna Karenina.

Scene

Perv #1: That got a Oprah sticker on it. It's got to be good and shit. Oprah, she smart.

Christoph: Yeah. It's excellent writing. It really is a classic. It is like the Deep Throat of novels.

Perv #2: So, who is this Anna Karenina bitch? Does she like the D?

Christoph: She does; that is the problem and the plot. She has a man, but she likes this other one.

Perv #2: He probably got that big dick.

Perv #3: He getting cucked or does he not know? What is the name of the guy she is fucking on the side?

Christoph: Count Vronsky.

Perv #1: Motherfucker's named Count Vronsky! Yeah, he definitely got that big dick. Bitches, in the end it is about giving them that good dick and hitting it right. It just the way it be.

Perv #2: It's true (he holds up a DVD of Blackzilla 18).

Christoph: Well, you might be on to something because back then cheating and divorce were things you just didn't do. So, Anna must have re- ally needed some Good D; Tolstoy never says it outright, but Anna's man Alexi probably does not deliver good penis.

Perv #3: Her nigga's name is Alexi? What kind of pussy name is that? No boy named Alexi is gonna hit it right.

Christoph: Um, sort of, but there is more going on. It ain't just about Anna Karenina, there is like a whole 'nother story going on with this guy named Levin who is really into and wants to marry this girl named Kitty. He keeps trying to get her to marry him while Anna keeps . . . trying to get the cock from the Count.

Perv #2: That Count Vronsky a straight player, can't hate on that motherfucker . . . But Kitty sounds like some virgin tight pussy, he needs to lock that pussy down. What's up with Levin; he not a baller?

Christoph: Um . . . I guess he is medium pimpin'?

Perv #3: You know, that ain't right. Medium, that should be good. I bet'cha Levin is a good man.

Christoph: You know, he is; he's got character. Definitely old-school values. Just wants to work the field and have a good woman.

Perv #2: Damn, that should be enough to get some quality pussy. Bitches want too much; ain't nothing changed. Shit ain't no different with them Russian motherfuckers. Pussy is the same everywhere.

Perv #3: That is true, I feel that shit; you work hard, you stable, but that ain't enough—bitches be acting stupid. I swear I see them either wanting broke ass niggas or ballers, but us middle men—we up inhere buying and renting this bullshit (he holds up AssParade 38).

Christoph: I hear ya, but in the book it takes some time for Kitty to see it but eventually she sees that Levin is the right man and they get married and he ends up happy.

Perv #3: That is good.

Perv #1: So what happened to the Anna Karenina ho?

Christoph: She kills herself.

Perv #1: Another bitch killed by the dick.

Perv #2: Ain't the first, ain't gonna be the last . . . Hey Christoph, ring me up.

POETRY

SATAN LOVES YOU: JOANNA C. VALENTE

A woman on the phone says she is dying
   turns thunder into a body that men

sing about, a bird of bones and breathe

who lived to see her three sons and husband

die, hung by a rope

a refraction of pink moon pooling
   over the tongues and wings of men like
   salted weeds and sea irises painted

blue because there is no life after

death and who actually believes
   in anything beyond what a dark tree

in the middle of a sea named Heaven
    could offer anyone but a distance

you call a run that fails you every time

because there are always calories
    and journals and ways to fill a thing called

a void with names you hear like music

in a bar after midnight where no one ever
    plays KISS because this is not the NJ

turnpike and this woman on the phone can't be

found anymore, not by a dial up
    modem, not by text

but still you come looking for her body

only to find there is no body and there is no

thunder, just lightning and a dial tone and
    an answer only in your head and some music

sheets to a song you hate.

All these years after her sons and her husband

to see the rope hiding in the tool shed, in

the backseat of your car and wherever she is,
    you write a letter to her, unsigned, stamped

a year too late.

It was never about the music.

THE LAMB AND THE WOLF: LOREN KLEINMAN

For Hélène Cixous

The wolf kisses the side of the lamb, and its head bends like the side of a paper cup. The wolf is hungry, wants the lamb in her belly.

Never let lamb go, never let it go.

I want to hold you in my mouth, says the wolf. *I want you to hold me in your mouth*, says the lamb.

They stare at each other. It doesn't matter who talks first.

Wolf rubs lamb's head, rubs her snout, cool-wet on the wool.

I want to eat you like a metaphor, says the wolf. *I want you to eat me*, says the lamb.

They stare at the moon, at the end of the farm, just the wolf and the lamb. Their teeth, sharp for each other.

FUCK YOUR FLAT EARTH, I WANT A HALLOW EARTH: SAM RICHARD

Fuck your flat earth,
Numbskull Theory,
With no imagination.
I want a hallow earth.
The planet's cavernous wound,
Writhing with ancient terrestrial creatures,
Unknowable and forgotten.
They evolved in darkness,
And the crushing weight,
Of the Earth's cold center.
When we dig too deep,
Scorched skin and burning eyes,
Befall the creatures that reign below.
I want to go there,
Exploring.
Excavating.
Spelunking.
Bringing back pieces,
Of them,
Of you,
Of us.
And in this ancestral house,
I will find peace.
Tranquility,
All silent but the sound of,

Massive centipedes,
Slurping the gelatinous brains,
From the skulls of my companions
And for the first time,
The only time,
In this wretched and horrible life,
I will know,
I am home.

WHY BEES STING (EVEN KNOWING WHAT WILL HAPPEN) KAT GIORDANO

i'm not talking about the wave of rage
that comes when one is cut off
in traffic, or buying groceries, that blip
of a primal urge to snap a neck,
disappearing too soon to be
rightfully acknowledged.
when she'd wound him,
disappearing at night to buy drugs
and re-emerge remorseless,
a hot-air gaslight full of bile
and fake babies, what i pictured
was not a cartoon death,
some kind of petty punchline.

i wanted
to tear each shred of flesh from her small body,
wanted her skin in ribbons through the cracks
in my fingers. a novice, lacking the right
vocabulary for violence, I pictured
clenching some vague organ,
relishing fistfuls of something crimson and soft.
in the old tradition, wasting nothing,
i'd floss the meat from my teeth with sinew,
my neck a carabiner keyring of bitch bones,
knowing all the while this vicious unwinding

of entrails like streamers from a sad piñata
is still a holier sacrament than she gave
him with this body, when it was still
a body.
when i could still wonder
why bees sting, even knowing
what will happen.

Just a pond of noise
in an ocean of silence
with drops of music.

My aunt: I hate her.
She is a fucking psycho
(in medical terms).

Red lifesavers that
float on the sea, red tombstones
we choose not to see.

BEHIND THE GENETIC REAPING:
STEPHANIE M. WYTOVICH

The world, a soon-to-be hospice,
brings with it a creature, a monster,
a culmination of everything less-than-desired,
an inactive participant, dormant, asleep;
yet there's a stewing in the after wake of medical nightmare,
this freak-show discovery,
this harbinger of mutation,
it waits in syringes-induced comas
hesitates in its failed posthumous abortion
for inside this genetic accident,
there exists the hardship of weakness,
an off-color, misbranded creation
that looks different than those around it;
a blinking taboo, a wheezing unmentionable
there's a crack in the system, a fraction in the plan

But, hear me, death-bed inhabitants!
Listen close: there's a reaper in your head.

A slave to the dominance of survival,
there's a cowering, a receding back to black,
a hanging in its suspended womb, this miscarriage-survived;
it was created to suffer, to duel out the agony of existence,
to force-feed humanity it's political agenda of hate;

like a well-oiled mechanical mutant,
it writhes in declination with each breath,
a recessive abomination, disease ridden and paled,
it feasts on your supply of white blood cells and hope,
a meat suit siphoned, a psychic heretic
it will eat you to survive, harvest you to laugh.

ISOLA: LISA MARIE BASILE

It is me, my king. I came in from the rain. We have been shuttered in, we listen to hail. Age is coming and you can see it in the distance. Water laces in beneath the glass quickly. Is it a poison or is it a dream? In the morning there is a blue wind. I have invoked it. I am the carrier of things and the things carry me. Oh, in this fortress I am not grieving. I am made of the things that I have chosen, and I have chosen the sea and things golden. I have chosen walls. It may seem painful, my king. It may seem as though I am standing out toward the light and praying for leave, but I am still and stillness is neither ache nor awe. I am in the midst of this place and it is the midst of me. It may seem daunting to be bled, to be in a place that cannot be contained, as though we have some right to contain things. It may seem God's revolt that we die, and cannot stand on balconies forever. It may seem cruel, but nature is sent to us to teach the story of terror and serenity. I have been the bloodlet and I have been the organ. I have understood the horses. I have died in the night. I have resurrected, my king. I would not rather be the cherub facing east. I am a new sort of gilded thing. I am the stillness of the grotesque, and a whole fortress of body and precipice. It can be neither desecrated nor worshipped. There is nothing here but nature tonight.

SELENA WAS 2 GOOD 4 U: LEZA CANTORAL

Selena was 2 good 4 u

but the heart wants what it wants
she was yours, body and soul

you had that pussy on lockdown
she laid it down
and you buried your face in stripper boobs
and drank sizzurp with rappers

your boyfriend video
is false advertising
cause you're a shitty boyfriend

no girl in her right mind
would eat fondue w u

MASOCHISM: B. DIEHL

You moved out 3 months ago —
and I feel like a stalker
because I still look at your Instagram all the time.
(A few days ago, I had a panic attack because
I accidentally "liked" one your photos from 2013.
Later, I had a second panic attack
when I realized you probably didn't even notice.)

I can't bring myself
to get rid of the junk you left behind.

A pair of your dirty socks are still in the corner.

And one of your earrings
is still on the nightstand:
a small, silver sparrow
with extended wings —
free and wild and untamed,
just like you were
on the night you left.

I can't let myself get over you.

I refuse to vacuum my bedroom rug

because it's packed with your hair.
There is so much of your hair in this house
that somehow, when I empty
my cat's litterbox, I see strands of it in his shit.

If I were to let myself get over you,
I would no longer have a motive, a purpose,

a reason to set an alarm clock
every night before bed.

That's why I still use your ashtray when I smoke.

That's why I still drink
from your blue coffee mug.

IT HAPPENED TO ME: I KISSED A GRAVEDIGGER: STEPHANIE VALENTE

we met on on ok cupid
i didn't know your
type of living

i was 25
& absent-minded

in truth,
you bored me

then, i heard
you made space
for the dead

i knew, i had to
for prosperity
for thrashing
for screaming
into grey moon light

because liking slayer
& ripped tee shirts at 19
wasn't enough

sorry, darling
i need street cred

my lips went ghostly
overripe & purple veined

in my dreams that night,
i pulled pulpy petals
out of my teeth

the next day,
i had to wear dark lipstick
to hide teeth marks
in little bloated shapes

girls at the office
asked if i got restalyne
i din't say no.

FUCK MUMFORD AND SONS: CHRIS ANTZOULIS

There are butchers
crawling up the street;
they were once living
in dank holes
that we covered
with amendments,
with shirts, ties, and pant
suits,
and just a thin layer of soil.
We planted seeds.
And we talked so much
the spittle made them grow.
But they could hear
when we lost
our
bite.
And so they pulled
at the roots,
tore the fabric
and ignored the language
after we misplaced
it's electricity.

And as the first one of us went

lip-to-lip
with a butcher,
we lead with a quiver
as they unfurled
in a wave of knives and torches.

BURIAL: ASHLEY INGUANTA

At a baseball game in Santa Fe, the prairie told me a secret. It was full, like lungs swelling with dirt, roots. I grabbed at it and ran into a vision of my father, the moon, uncurling a rope for me; I run up into his light, and he's telling me All girls grow, all girls grow, and the air is soft—like Prairie's hands, like my breathing—and it is then I understand why dogs walk on all fours, why our legs are important, why I said yes when she crawled inside of my mouth, scared and hiding like a sheep, wanting me to rescue her, lovingly, like Mary did; but I am not Mary I say, and my father, he is still there, large and glowing moon, and my body—my body is heavy stone sinking water, food for sheep, clay apple, and I believe Prairie when she touches me, her fingers sliding deep into my body, a wish for me to become, become. I believe Prairie when she says, Shhh, girl, and when she says, No one knows how beautiful the sky is here. No one. But we know. I touch Prairie's cheek, she hums, her throat as worn as a dog's. My legs are sore. I look up and see purple, red—falling onto the moon, falling onto her hands—and the rope my father uncurled, it's loose now, swinging; and my body, it's growing, and I don't stop it. I run far, far away from this sky no one but we three have seen. I am heavy with water, with roots. My feet are big as satellites. I will not tell a thing. Not a thing.

THIS TENDER THING: DANIEL KNAUF

She very carefully plucks

The dying blossoms

From the potted flower

Collecting them in her palm

Leaving the sparse few

Their color tawdry

And fragile.

Without meeting my eyes

She places them in my palm

Their stems damp and

Chill, and gestures toward

The rubbish bin.

I walk to it

A few feet from the hallowed ground

Which swaddles the bones

Of her son and now

His father.

I watch in reverent awe

As she reaches

Into a plastic tote

And withdraws a soft rag

And a spray bottle

Of blue cleaning fluid.

I watch in reverent awe

As she cleanses the polished stone

With the same patient, methodical care

I have seen her sponge the surfaces

Of her kitchen

After a meal.

I watch in reverent awe

As she collects a broom

From its customary spot under a willow

And sweeps the gravel

Surrounding the stone

Erasing our footprints.

She steps back and appraises

Her work.

Satisfied, she turns to me

And meets my eyes.

I give her a very slight nod.

She smiles, seeing that I understand

And approve.

This tender thing.

Returns the rag and the Windex

Into the bag.

I take her in my arms

And only then does she falter.

Her tears dampen my coat.

I kiss the top of her head,

This woman

This mother

This wife

This tender thing.

FICTION

THE ANARCHIST KOSHER COOKBOOK:
MAXWELL BAUMAN

1. This recipe was passed down from my Bubbe for when law and order goes out the window. Can you hear the mob of skinheads getting closer? Their fiery, nationalist chants echo in the streets. What's there left for you to do? Get cooking of course.

2. This isn't the time to fry up some latkes, but inside this cookbook are the secrets for those hungry for revolution. These are the secrets to craft a protector for yourself in the same ancient way that God used to craft Adam. This guardian is known as the golem.

3. The first thing you'll need for your golem is clay. Go down to the riverbank and with your bare hands scoop up a bucket full of virgin soil. Be careful to sort out any pebbles or rocks. At sunset, submerge the dirt into a pot of boiling water and stir. Pour the mud onto a plate that has never been touched by meat and dairy at the same time. Take seven tablespoons of Kosher salt, one for the tears shed over each day of creation, and kneed it into the dirt.

4. You won't be using this clay to make a golem from scratch. You can use the remains of an old, shattered golem instead. You can find the parts of old golems in the attic of any synagogue. It'll be in the box labeled "Xmas Decorations."

5. Gather the broken pieces and use the clay to bind the shards together like a giant puzzle. You'll find that each golem will have its own look, style, and amount of detail. Don't be

thrown off by the level of anatomical accuracy. While we come from a people that pride themselves on their modesty, the hands that first crafted the golem went the extra mile to display its circumcision with pride.

6. Once the golem has its form, straddle it and rest your mouth against the golem's and repeat, "Yahweh, Adonoi, Elohim" over and over again until you lips move so fast that you appear like a drunk, mumbling lunatic. If the fear of God is in your heart, the creature will stir. You may be unaware that the life has entered the creature until its erect member pokes into your groin.

7. Give the golem tasks by writing a command on a piece of paper, roll it up into a scroll and insert it into its mouth. But you must always be specific and not give it an impossible task. You shouldn't tell it to go off and kill all the skinheads because then it will go out and try to kill every skinhead in the world. It won't get very far, let alone make much a dent in your current problem.

8. Be explicit with what you want your golem to do. The golem needs clear targets. Learn when and where the skinheads will be. Timing will be key to your success. Aim for early in the morning before daybreak while they're still outside and drunk. Wait until one is alone. You can have the golem push the skinhead into traffic, off a bridge or into a trash compactor.

9. It will be tempting to mutilate them every time because they deserve whatever pain they get and then some. But too many grand displays will make the skinheads suspicious. If you keep the attacks strategic, they will blame their friends' deaths on inebriation, but you'll know better.

10. When not crushing windpipes or throwing Neo Nazi's in the river, it is important to keep the golem busy with any kind of task. Any assignment will do. Have it cook, clean, and balance your checkbook. If the golem is left with too much down time, it will find a way to occupy itself.

11. The golem will sit next to you and take your hand in his. It will loop its arm around the small of your back and draw you in close. It will stroke your hair and nibble on your neck. The golem will scoop you up and carry you to the bed. It will slowly undress you and cup your breasts or buttocks. Its

fingers will travel over your curves and spread your legs, and nosh the night away.

12. This newfound taste for pleasure will consume the golem's mind and start ignoring your orders. Then it will require discipline.

13. If your golem disregards your commands then you will have to reestablish dominance. You can't simply punish it like a child by taking away its toys because it has no sense of ownership. And you can't treat it like a bad dog by hitting it on the snout with a newspaper because that's just silly. You'll have to take more drastic measures if you want to see results.

14. Grab the golem by its hefty cock and balls. Tell it that this is what happens when your instructions are snubbed. Take an icepick and chisel off its manhood until it's as smooth as a department store mannequin. You could either lock its genitals in your junk drawer as just another tchotchke, or you can throw them on the floor and smash them into dust with your heel to really drive your point home. Either way, this will put the golem back in line. Remember: A little castration goes a long way.

15. No matter where you are, the neighbors love to gossip. Some have mentioned seeing a strange man coming and going at odd hours of the night. They want details about the new man in your life. It's not like you can be direct with them about the golem. If they knew, they'd want to use it for themselves and there's no guarantee that their goals are as selfless as yours.

16. And what are you to do if the neighbors, yenting around, become aware of the golem, or the skinheads track down the source of the thing killing off their Anti-Semitic allies?

17. So the skinheads have found you out. They've circled your house and are throwing their Molotov Cocktails. You have two choices of how to respond.

18. You can send the golem right out the front door to defend your home. Now is your opportunity to let the golem go wild. It'll rip apart limbs. The golem is strong and can take a beating, but risks being overwhelmed.

19. Your only other option you have is to run. The golem will cradle you in its arms and dash you outside and push through

the angry mob. It will protect you from your pursuers, but you must keep moving.

20. Returning home isn't an option. If you are lucky, you'll be able to stay a day or two ahead of your pursuers. You won't be able to stay in one place for long.

21. Even though the golem has helped you escape, when it comes down to it, it is also holding you back from moving ahead. It's simple for an old lady to disappear in a crowd, but it's nearly impossible with such a massive figure drawing attention. While you can dress up the golem, give it a big hat and shades, but people will know that something is off. The only way for you to truly vanish is to get rid of the golem.

22. You may have grown attached to it after all you two have gone through together. It was a protector, a lover, and maybe even a friend. If you thought it would be bad if your neighbors took control of the creature, just imagine the ensuing nightmare if the skinheads bent it to their twisted will.

23. Put one last scroll in the golem's mouth instructing it to remain still. Take something heavy like a mallet or lead pipe and approach the creature from behind. Strike the golem with all your strength. Keep hitting it until only fractured remains and tiny scrolls are left. You can gather the scrolls and burn them.

24. Put the golem's shattered pieces in a box and label it "Xmas Decorations" and leave it on the doorstep of the closest synagogue. They'll know what to do with it.

FINGER PRINTS ON THE BLIND TOUR: MADELEINE SWANN

Billie always woke first, giving her extra time to worry about rape, and her. She always checked her phone, heading straight for Twitter. Today, all the moments were in Italian, so at least there were no shrieking headlines or arguments to read through. She still searched the tweets of those she followed, though, to see if anyone mentioned them.

Each new perpetrator or speaker of misjudged comments, their unsuspecting publicity shot framing an accusation, filled her with fear, rage and crushing doom. Each new #soandsoisoverparty and #soandsoiscancelled tweet was a tiny tentacle pulling her down into the filthy depths. Anyone with resentment could make a claim against anyone. It was a witch hunt.

Was it? She'd think that for a few seconds before reading the accuser's words and feeling like the worst person alive for doubting. No, it wasn't a witch-hunt, it was revolution. Things were changing for the better, this was necessary. She had plenty of #metoo stories of her own, from the man who pinched her 14 year old behind at the swimming pool to sexual harassment at work to the boyfriend who woke her up humping her. Several times. She still burned with anger at that. No, this was more like the English Civil War than a witch-hunt. Sure, some Puritans might take things too far, but the majority of people just wanted equality.

But didn't she belong among the accused? No, with the accusers. But...

Round and round she went like this every morning and today was no different, despite not being able to read new stories. She looked down at Sam's serene, sleeping face and boiled with jealousy. He could sleep through a nuclear war. Immediately she felt bad and thanked whatever made them go to the same café every Sunday morning five months ago. The hole she had fallen down was so dark she couldn't see the sign posts, as her mother would have said, and she'd decided to get a nice man to protect her from herself. And there he was, Sam, torch in hand. He invited her in like a stray cat, didn't pull back when she cried without explanation or ask in harsh tones what the matter was now. He didn't question her when she went out all night or hid her phone when reading certain texts. She in turn held onto him tightly, keen to block out the previous night's kisses with strangers, or worse.

Sam's eyes fluttered open. "Hello," Billie pulled him close.

"I'm like a weird pirate," he said. Billie frowned in confusion before noticing her boob covering his eye. They laughed and kissed, Billie enjoying his musty smell.

"I could sit on your shoulder like a parrot."

"And say 'aw' and stroke my hair every time I tell people to walk to the plank." He got up to check the itinerary, "Uffizi gallery this morning, Fairy," he said, using her pet name as naturally as her given one.

"OK," she grumbled, unwillingly leaving the hotel bed and pulling her clothes on. He admonished her while she danced about like a child but he was laughing. When she was finally ready he unfurled his blind stick and they headed onto the beige streets of Florence. They passed market stalls selling colourful scarves and trinkets and sign after sign of Renaissance exhibitions. She felt the art seep into her pores and replace her toxic blood. She gripped Sam's hand and he smiled at her so sweetly that she almost burst into tears. Get a grip, she told herself, when did you become such a sap? She ignored the voice reminding her that she had always been a sap and no amount of pretending otherwise would change that. "Shall I check where the gallery is?"

"No, we'll find it, Florence isn't too big."

"I'll look," Billie pulled her phone from her pocket, trying to appear casually curious, a free spirit, not a person who panicked at the mere thought of aimless wandering. She couldn't help it, she went onto Twitter first. She scrolled for a few moments then stopped, horror shooting through her. The girl was there, her tweet hanging like rotten fruit among flowers, a retweet by a mutual friend. She was back. What had she said? "Thursday morning pick me up," above a picture of a fruit smoothie. Billie wanted to go back to the room. No, she wanted to go back to England. No, she wanted to die.

"Alright?"

"Yeah," she found the Uffizi and dropped a pin, slipping her arm through Sam's and leading him through the plaza past statues of Gods and Biblical characters. They located the entrance and joined the queue, eventually arriving at some marble stairs. Billie guided Sam onto the first step.

"Scusa," called a voice, and Billie didn't catch the rest. A woman in a uniform stood by a lift and she caught on, guiding Sam towards her.

"That was handy," said Sam once they reached the top, and Billie almost burst into tears at how innocently happy he was. He was pure, his life unblemished. She squeezed his arm and laid her head on his shoulder. They wandered slowly through a room filled with beautiful nude women and stern royalty when another gallery worker approached them.

"If you like, we can lead you on a special tour where you can touch certain statues?" He glanced down at Sam's stick.

"Oh, it's fine, I can see a small tunnel in front of me." Billie tried to back him up but the man, urgent in his need to help, didn't seem to hear. "OK then," said Sam, and Billie thought if she stared at him hard enough he would hear her objections. He didn't, and pulled on the white gloves handed to him. They were trapped in their own politeness.

"This way," he led them to the first statue, a woman lying on her side. He seemed so pleased Billie couldn't bear to disappoint him. Awkwardly Sam followed his instructions, reaching out and caressing a statue he could see perfectly well. The guide read out the plaque beneath.

On they went to the next, traipsing past staring visitors, Billie's shoes echoing off the walls and floor, until they reached a nude marble man. Again Sam reached out to the marble figure. Billie sidled up beside him and leaned into his ear, "Just touch their dicks, he might think we're weird and leave."

"Shh," Sam fought against laughter, his face turning red. Guiltily continued, his concentration doubling. The guide was still reading the carved text and Billie held in a sigh. How long was this going to go on for? Should they say something after all? She opened her mouth to speak when Sam's phone beeped in his pocket. It was the Twitter noise. Billie let go of his arm, afraid he would notice her fear. She clasped her hands, her knuckles turning a sickly pale.

"No," she said, stopping him from reaching for it, "look after, when we're finished."

"OK," he kissed her nose, "sorry, Fairy." She hoped he didn't notice the tears threatening to erupt.

The tour continued, the guide reading words they had both already read, describing statues they could both see, Sam looking as politely bored as before. Billie wanted it to continue forever. Here, locked in the boredom of a useless tour, she was safe. Sam wouldn't read the message that had to be from the girl, and Billie's life wouldn't change in horrific ways. Images flashed in her mind; going home with the girl, a friend of a friend, after meeting in a club. The girl making the first move...no, she'd made the first move. Had she? She didn't know. For hours they'd sloppily tried to make each other orgasm, too drunk to feel much of anything, but the girl was beautiful and Billie had just enjoyed looking at her. Eventually they both collapsed beside each other, giggling, before falling into an alcoholic slumber.

The next morning the girl had insisted she had too much to do for Billie to hang around and they'd barely looked at each other. Still she thought nothing of it until weeks later as she walked home from work. The girl was parked in her car, and she noticed Billie in her rear view mirror and turned to look out her open window. That look was branded on Billie's eyelids. The outrage in the parted lips, the accusation in her stare, the horror and confusion it stirred in Billie. From that point on her life was over. They never saw each other again and the girl disappeared from Twitter...but now she was back.

Looming over them was a stone bearded man, or at least that's what Billie had thought. When Sam moved his hand, though, she saw a finger print. "Careful," she pointed, "that one's not ready yet." Sam looked up, lip curled in amusement.

"That's right," he said in the voice they used when pretending the other was a simpleton, "it hasn't been in the oven long enough, has it?" Sam pretended to laugh but her body shook as he left more and more handprints neither he nor the guide seemed to notice.

The same thing happened at the next, and the next. The sculpted arm of a baby in its mother's embrace noticeably lowered. "Did you see?" Billie couldn't finish, instead pointing lamely at the drooping limb.

"What, sweetheart?"

"Uh, nothing." Sam turned back and the baby's arm dropped to the floor with a wet clay slap. Billie stared at the grey puddle on the floor. She wanted to talk, to scream, to tell him everything right from the start.

"Are you OK?" Sam was at her side, hands on her shoulders, looking into her eyes. They were so soft and kind. She didn't deserve him. It took her a few seconds to realise she'd toppled into the wall. "I've got to take her back," the guide agreed, face stern with worry.

"I show you out the back way."

Sam started after him, his hand in hers. Billie didn't move. "Come on," he was trying to stay calm, she could tell, "it's OK." She shuffled slowly after him.

The guide led them to the lift, Sam holding her tightly all the way down. Billie clutched his arm, certain she was leaving nail marks and not caring. The doors slid open and they made their way through double doors into a long, silent corridor. Dust sprinkled into the air with every step and paintings covered in white cloths or brown paper leaned against the walls. The smell of old attics tickled Billie's nose hairs, reminding her of happier times reading her book in the loft as a child. On they went, the end of her world waiting just outside.

It was so quiet, she couldn't even hear the people in the main queue, wherever they were. On and on they trudged, eyes forward. The dust settled, no longer choking the air, as if their feet had no weight. The smell faded and Billie walked taller, her heart slowing. She was no longer afraid. The guide didn't look back, didn't speak, just kept walking and they kept following. She slipped her arm through Sam's. He didn't turn to her or acknowledge it but she didn't mind. She didn't care if they never spoke again as long as they were here where it was safe. They kept walking. They kept walking.

This morning, while waiting for a bus in Bogotá, an old woman saw me writing in my notebook and told me to record her story. She held a basket of round, red fruits. She started with a sigh.

"When I was your age, *mija,* I had my heart broken by a beautiful man. He was handsome and spoke like a poet. He loved me thoroughly and then left our *pueblito* for the city, and never returned.

"My father was a *maracuyá* farmer. You know passionfruit, with its thick rind and tartness. The night my heart broke, I was slicing *maracuyás* to make juice. Back then we didn't have a blender—we did everything by hand. My hands and the hands of my sisters were always sticky from pressing juice.

"That night I was weeping all over the fruit. The ache in my chest was terrible and I wanted to get rid of it. So I took a big *maracuyá* and opened it with a clean cut from the blossom-end up. I scraped out the thick pulp with a spoon, and rinsed the shell clean.

"And then, *mija*—" the old woman leaned close—"I opened my chest. I made a little scratch with the knife's tip, and it didn't even hurt. Nothing could be worse than that pain in my heart. I peeled my flesh from the cut and reached between my ribs to where my heart was hanging, split in two equal parts. I unhooked one half, not squeezing too hard, and placed it inside the empty *maracuyá* shell. Then I stitched my chest back up with red thread, using honey to stick the two halves of the fruit together. I licked the seam clean. That night I buried it under the tallest *maracuyá* tree in our orchard.

"That was fifty years ago," the old woman said. "And now, *mira.*"

She pressed one of the red fruits from her basket into my hand. *Maracuyás* are usually yellow or green on the outside, but this one was red. The old woman grinned. She leaned closer, glanced around us, and unfastened two buttons of her blouse. There was a thin scar over her left breast.

"Yes, *mija,*" she said, "it's possible to survive your whole life with just half a heart."

A bus roared up and the old woman gestured that it was hers. Mouth dry, all I could say was *gracias, abuela.* The bus disappeared in a choke of diesel smoke. The fruit was warm in my hands. It began to rain.

Now, after dinner, I slice the red fruit with a knife. It splits into two equal parts. Usually *maracuyá* pulp is a mix of yellow, grey, or orange, but this one is blood-crimson and the seeds are a vicious red-black, like clots. I spoon out a mouthful. It tastes familiar, but richer than any *maracuyá* I've had before. It's almost saline—like passion fruit mixed with honey and salt. The aftertaste is metallic. My own heart pounds as I swallow every bite down.

CATCH YOU ON THE FLIP SIDE: CHARLES AUSTIN MUIR

I. Self

SOPHISTICATED SIPS E-ZINE

Full-bodied flash fiction for the online lit lover

Our electronic word java will stoke your cyber-soul. Grab a seat and let our signature blends transport you from your reading device to a psychic realm where a woman's laugh drives you insane and a bus ride takes you to the end of the night. We add flavor and finish to what T.S. Eliot called "the substratum of our being." And we will measure your life in coffee spoons.

Today's digital dose of belletristic brew:

SELF-PORTRAIT

By George Kuato

"God, look at that portrait," Lewis said.

"You talk as if it's horrid," Sylvia said.

"It's more than horrid. It's positively hideous. He's a swine in gentleman's clothes."

"Perhaps you're being harsh."

"Harsh? Humor me, Sylvia; try to see it through my eyes. Eyes…now that's where to start. How they glare at you, how they swipe at you like a scythe. Do you see it? The forehead taut, as if pricked with damnation; the horn of a beard, and the bushy brows that meet in the middle. That's damnation enough. And the bulbous nose that gives the face the shape of—why, you can almost hear him snorting, like an overgrown hog. Walk over this way; he's still staring at you. I think he would like to eat you."

"Stop it," Sylvia whispered, lowering her head.

"He must have been massive," Lewis pressed on, "so massive he stoops under his own weight. And wonderfully cunning in the effect he wished to produce. He had the picture hung at such a height over the landing so as to appear from below as though the master of the house himself, bandy-legged and huge in his black frock coat and top hat, were standing there measuring you with carnivorous lust.

"I have read of this man," he continued, slowing near the foot of the stairs, "a recluse who was disposed to treat his menials savagely in the fever-grip of drunkenness. I can imagine him, Sylvia (here—sit on this bench), hulking into classrooms at Edinburgh and thundering on the marvelous unbosomings of the human corpse. He would terrify me and fascinate me all the same. I shouldn't think I could take my eyes off him."

"Oh, Lewis, can't we go back to the sitting room?"

"And listen to Polly's dreadful piano? Please, you're trying to observe with the same liberal consciousness that delights in your garden. Try to view the painting my way, like a cave dweller who perceives his own shadow in the gloom. For in my vision each shadow stands distinctly revealed, the shadow behind every shard of existence, preying on its own kind, mocking itself… But enough metaphysics. Back to the picture: Help me build it. Note the features, how they burn themselves on your mind's eye whether you regard the subject directly or not. They have a kind of sordid musical elegance about them which exhausts the limits of the grotesque. Our man is like a monstrous violin with a beard —no, no, that certainly won't do. He's like the shadow of a satyr in one of Baudelaire's brothels; no, wait a minute, rather like the creeping arm of the Marquis De Sade's nude, drooling ghost—"

"Lewis, please stop!"

He sighed, and sat on the bench beside her.

"You're only trying to provoke me," she said. "No man would allow himself to be depicted so."

"Ah, but I'm merely dispensing with the trivialities of, shall we say, surface delineation; speaking in truths of the heart."

"His heart? Is it so black, do you think?"

"I do think, Sylvia. Such a man has been stung by the viciousness of his peers. You can tell that—assuming the artist has been faithful—by the stamp of vengefulness on his brow. Left there in childhood, I would argue, for surely it would have taken him years to grow into those prominent features, which would have drawn accusations of wickedness in his youth. So that he would play the devil for survival's sake and find the role an unshakable one, even into adulthood."

"Then it's all a defense," she countered, "to close off an emptiness that might be filled by a loving woman."

He smiled, looking from her to the landing. "And that is why you captivate me, my dear: Those God-given lenses upon your face that allow you to spot a crack of light in even the darkest corners of the spirit. Yes, perhaps love might have worked on this man once."

"He doesn't seem so ugly now," she said.

There was a moment of silence.

"But look," he broke out, turning to her, his eyes shining: "Beware, Sylvia, lest your scrupulous self-regard, your romantic invulnerability (which few, I dare say, have glimpsed beneath that haze of beneficence about you) should rouse that twisted creature on the landing, so that one day, one day he steps down from the portrait and with a noise like chunks of masonry hoisted with each step —*thump, thump, thump*— drooling like a fiendish monk—comes banging on your chamber door —"

She shrieked as his hand clamped on her arm.

"You're insufferable, Lewis," she said, rising.

"Am I? I was swept away by my conceit."

"I don't know why I play along with your games. They always end in some cruel joke."

With a barely audible huff she brushed her arm where he had touched her.

Then, with the hauteur of a dancer recovering from an inferior partner's stumble, she thrust out her elbow and waited; so remote and so beautiful, he thought, like a prisoner in a tower of gossamer and lace sculpted from ice.

He frowned, stroking his beard; then stood.

"Thanks to my 'scrupulous self-regard' as you call it," she said as they linked arms, "I asked Polly for a tour of the place before you came here. *And I know there is no portrait, but only a stained glass window on the landing.* A ballet of light and color so dazzling in her account of it that I ached to experience it as others do. Leave it to you, Lewis, to transform a celestial vision into something horrible for one who cannot see. Truths of the heart indeed."

And so saying she allowed the broad, bowed man to guide her down the hall.

II. Portrait

"It started off nicely," Brandon said. "But then it went on too long about how horrible the guy was. Overblown writing."

"Agreed," Keira said. "The writer could have trimmed some. But you've got to admit the twist ending was good."

"But was Lewis deliberately being cruel to Sylvia? Or just having a little fun to his way of thinking?" Vanessa scowled at her papers as she posed this to the Northwest Flash Fiction Freakazoids.

Consisting of nine aspiring writers at its peak, the group now stood at four. They met on campus as their schedules allowed to "dissect the use of brevity in the works of underpublished and emerging authors transmitting in all genres." Luke, the only published member, hated the smug, often over-long meetings. And yet he was the only Freakazoid who had attended every one.

Vanessa. His only motivation for enduring Brandon's discourses on Philip K. Dick. For making it to Medieval Literature every Tuesday and Thursday at eight in the morning. Half Irish, half Korean, she caught him off guard whenever she looked at him. Her curious brown eyes, so dark they seemed black, made him feel like a lumbering idiot, yet capable of change, as if he might emerge from his black-trench-coat-wearing, three-hundred-pound chrysalis to become someone semi-attractive, even desirable. Although he still wouldn't stand a chance with her.

Her romantic invulnerability.

"I think the story is deeper than it looks," he said. "It's all subtext, like Vanessa suggests."

"I'm not sure I'm suggesting that," Vanessa said.

Humor me, Vanessa; try to see it through my eyes.

"Yeah, Luke, clarify."

Luke turned to Keira across the table. But his attention burned around the dream girl at the edge of his vision, a tantalizing vagueness like a naked woman flitting through a moonlit forest.

He cleared his throat.

"What I mean is, the style reflects the man's extravagant way of speaking to conceal his self-hatred. It's no coincidence the story reads like *The Picture of Dorian Gray*."

"I think you're mistaking the author's long-windedness for characterization," Brandon said.

And I think you should eat Philip K. Dick's ass, you swine in Mr. Rogers clothes.

But before Luke could voice this opinion more tactfully, his cell phone dinged.

"Get home if you're not already," read the incoming text message preview on his lock screen. Luke Sr., the deus ex machina of malcontent Freakazoids. "Well guys, it looks like I've been summoned."

"Laters," Brandon said.

"Peace," Keira said.

"Catch you on the flip side, Luke," Vanessa said, not looking up as she shuffled her papers.

"So much for George Kuato," Luke heard from Keira as he lingered a moment outside the classroom.

He stared at his size-13 combat boots as he rode the bus home.

So much for George Kuato was right. He shouldn't have submitted his story to the group under false pretenses. A literary vignette like "Self-portrait"—despite its publication in an esteemed online litmag—was bound to leave the others cold. In Dewey Hall in Room 213 whenever the four could meet, depth took a backseat to plot twists and outrageous concepts. The girls thought he was hot shit ever since he took Advanced Fiction Writing. With Brandon leading the meetings, even Henry Miller would fall flat.

Another rub was the group's digital skimming habits. Vanessa was the only one besides Luke who read hard copy. And even she only vaguely sensed what "George Kuato" had accomplished. In under a thousand words, Luke's poetic double had used dialogue almost exclusively to depict a man's inner conflict and create irony and exaggeration so potent that it seemed as if the story was overwritten when really it illuminated the dark corners of Lewis's spirit.

Look into the dark corners of my spirit, Vanessa.

The retracting pneumatic bus doors sounded like a sigh.

Luke walked the five blocks from the bus stop to his house. The foyer still smelled of last night's ruined quiche, as well as the beef ravioli his dad had heated up after dumping Luke's experiment in the garbage. Luke Sr., the deus ex machina of Chef Boyardee. He hurried up the stairs. His dad's work boots—size 13s, like his—weren't by the coat rack, which meant he still had a few minutes to surf porn.

Down in the living room, Paula stopped her daily torture marathon of "Ode to Joy" on the Steinway to catch her brother's tread on the landing. The stained-glass window there, with its yellows and blues and reds refracting midafternoon sunlight, so frightening after he watched *Suspiria* when he was ten, now only made him squint into its geometric conundrum impatiently. He locked himself in his room and plopped into his chair at his desktop computer.

His cell phone dinged. "Hitching a ride in five," read the incoming text message preview. The old man's daytime texts were as terse as his evening diatribes were expansive. Another ding. "Make dinner. No vegetarian."

Luke silenced his cell phone. Time to pull up his online obsession—Lillian Chong.

She was Vanessa's dead ringer on SploogeTube, only borderline anorexic. His favorite video of her was a POV, a dude with Lou Ferrigno forearms giving her a vaginal cream pie. The HD stream made it easy for him to fall into the illusion of banging Lillian Chong missionary style. Whenever Luke masturbated to the video, fighting for leverage against his big thighs and belly—like giving a polar bear a reach-around—the porn star would morph in his mind's eye. She would become Vanessa, legs spread wide, nipples needle-stiff, totally going Freakazoid under his vicarious Incredible Hulk thrusts.

"Oh God, Vanessa," Luke would rasp in hoarse delight, as "Ode to Joy" screeched through the floor like a tone-deaf cheer and sperm shot past the Angel Soft toilet tissue he pressed to his dick to slick a crevice (once even the Apple logo on his monitor) in his keyboard.

And that is why you captivate me, my dear.

While he accessed the website, he imagined a text from her.

"I knew it was your story," punctuated with a winking eye and stuck-out tongue emoji. "Only you would write such a deep, sexy piece and then credit it with an Arnold Schwarzenegger movie reference. Ha ha, Kuato. I love-love-LOVE *Total Recall*. But I love you even more, Luke, I wish you were here with me. I want you deep inside me."

The POV video took time loading. Dimly visible, Luke's reflection stared back at him from the black monitor.

I'm starting to look like Dad, he thought. Someday I'll look just like him.

His monobrow furrowed.

Vanessa—is this what you see when you look at me?

Could you spot a crack of light in the dark corners of my spirit?

Catch you on the flip side, Luke.

The repulsive face faded as the video finally began playing. But an impressionistic ghost remained, arrested behind Lillian Chong's rolling eyes and protruding ribs. Luke grabbed his sperm wipe and brutalized his cock. Yes, you will, Vanessa, he thought, as his sylvan goddess emerged from her Lillian Chong chrysalis in the zone of illusion between the flat screen in front of him and his synapses.

You'll catch me on the flip side, Vanessa.

When I step down from the portrait and come banging on your chamber door.

FROGSLAYER REX: JAYAPRAKASH SATYAMURTHY

The boy takes a shortcut to the bus stop. He follows a trail down a slope behind a cluster of houses, between several empty, overgrown lots, another cluster of houses and then the main road, where he crosses and is finally at the bus stop.

It is the rainy season, and the trail is muddy, waterlogged in places. This is when frogs come hopping. Small, dirt-coloured things. He is unsettled by their black, staring eyes. Their legs, so muscular—like they could leap right onto him...he stifles a gut-level shudder and tries to think about something else. When it's wet like this, he walks a little faster — not too fast because he has to be careful about splattering his school shoes—and breathes a little easier when he reaches the bus stop.

Sometimes he comes home later than usual because of tuitions. On those evenings, he takes a different, longer route because the trail is dark and scary at that time. Just once, he took the trail back in the evening. It was deserted and he tormented himself with the fantasy of a giant frog, glistening in the drizzle, huge hind legs bulging with muscles, following him quietly. It had felt so real he was afraid to look behind him.

One morning, a frog hops into his path, nearly under his feet (he thinks for a moment about the frog crunching, squelching underfoot and feels ill). A movement to the left distracts him. He turns to look, sees a green snake swallowing another frog. Its head is in the snake's mouth but the legs stick out, twitching. He tries to leave in two directions at once, slips and falls. The first frog hops up next to his face. He screams.

This attracts some children in the cluster of houses further down. They come running, two boys and a girl, a few years older than him. They see him, see the snake, assume that's what's spooked him. They hoot and throw stones at it until it slithers away, one froggy foot still sticking out of its mouth. One of the boys helps him up. The frog near the boy's face has disappeared. He mumbles thanks, sets off down the trail, spooked and embarrassed.

The next morning, he can't face taking the trail. He takes the long route, and winds up late at school. He is lined up with the other late students, given two strokes of the cane on his palms and sent off to classes. His palms sting all day and he decides not to go to school at all until the rains stop and the trail dries up.

The next day he loafs around, past the houses and the sun temple, across the rice paddies and into the barrens around the military firing range. There are many gullies and shallow canyons here, and no bushes for frogs to hide in. He deposits his schoolbag in a hidey-hole and runs around imagining adventures in his head. He sneaks close to the firing range, hoping to catch a glimpse of the soldiers and their guns, maybe in the midst of target practice.

He sees four soldiers in a small stand of trees. Two of them are standing, grinning. One bending over the fourth who is kneeling, bottom in the air. Before he quite registers the scene, the third soldier looks a bit like a big frog, squatting, his legs curved with muscle, like a frog's. Suddenly the boy realises what he is seeing. 'Ohhh. Buttsex.' And also, 'great I finally see sex happening and it's all guys'.

The soldiers have spotted him. The one who was humping the other disengages, comes chasing the boy, pants still down, face flushed, mouth spewing curses, something large and snake-like rampant between his legs. The boy runs, quick through the muddy barrens, his size an advantage as he darts through narrow gullies, recovers his bag and makes it to the first row of houses that marks the beginning of his neighbourhood. The soldiers have fallen back, and he is safe.

The boy gets home. It is too early to show himself. He shimmies up a coconut tree onto the roof, where he takes his own penis out of his pants and looks at it, wondering if it will ever be like the thing between the soldier's legs. He looks up to see a circle of frogs closing in on him. They stick their tongues out, and their tongues are snakes. He zips up his pants, shimmies back down and rings the doorbell. Makes some excuse for being home an hour early, spends the evening shaken and very quiet.

He takes the long way to the bus stop the next few days, doesn't think of skipping school. The soldiers may remember his face, may be looking out for him. One day at school he sees some older boys torturing cockroaches. They blast at them with a cockroach spray tube, then use a lit cigarette lighter to ignite the spray. This sets the cockroaches on fire. 'This would work on the frogs', the boy thinks.

Back home, he steals insect sprays from the cupboard below the kitchen sink and cigarette lighters from his father's bedside table. He cannibalises old t-shirts and an old gym bag to make a bullet belt holding spray cans and lighters. He fashions a handkerchief into a bandana and, with a red marker, scrawls a title on it: Frogslayer Rex.

Late at night, once his parents are snoring, he straps the belt across his chest, wraps the bandana around his head, paints black stripes of shoe polish on his cheeks and sneaks out. He heads to the trail, and is waiting for them to show themselves when he hears a weird groaning. He moves closer to its source.

At first, he thinks it is a giant frog. Then he realises it is a man with military fatigues down low around his ankles, squatting over someone else. 'Is that all these soldiers do, bugger each other', he thinks to himself, then realises the one moaning isn't a soldier. She is the girl who helped chase the snake away. He gasps. The soldier hears it, spots the boy and runs for him, face twisted in rage.

The boy has no time to think. He shakes a spray can and lets loose, holding a lit lighter in the spray. Fire hits the solider, right between the legs. Pubes on fire, the soldier screams, falls over and thrashes on the damp ground, trying to put out the flames. The boy runs to the girl, pulls out the sock the soldier has stuffed in her mouth. She screams her father's name. People come running. The girl tells them the whole story. Someone puts the soldier's crotch out then a whole lot of them beat him up. Civilian and military police show up. There is a lot of talking.

At some point, the boy finds himself sitting on a boulder, no one firing questions at him or heaping praises on him. There is a pressure on one of his feet. He looks down. It is a frog, looking up at him. He picks it up, deposits it off the trail, where it hops away. If a snake finds it, so be it. And if not, that too. He removes his improvised bandana, looks at the title he had scrawled on it. He crumples it up, stuffs it into a pocket. The sun is starting to show. At some point, he has to go home. Right now, he just savours the fact that there are less monsters in the world than the previous day.

VIDEOGAME GUY UPSTAIRS: SAM PINK

I.

The guy who used to live right above me played videogames a lot—sometimes for consecutive days, real loud during all times of the day.

He'd yell at the videogames and break things in his apartment while playing.

He'd yell, "Fucking goddamn stupid bullshit" and stomp on the floor a lot then there'd be a scary sound of something breaking/him screaming.

I liked him.

He was very creative with his swearing.

His swearing was always new and bold.

Like, it was always some variation of "fuck" with "shit" or "goddamn."

Like, "Fucking goddamn bullshit motherfucker I shot that motherfucker in the head."

Or, "Fucking bullshit, I blew that asshole up with a fucking mother*fucking* grenade."

His stomping was also impressive.

Seemed genuine, full of anger.

I felt the anger in each stomp.

If I had to guess, I'd say his stomps involved both feet at the same time, throwing his upper body backwards.

If I had to guess, I'd say his stomps involved imaginary heads beneath both feet.

And blood.

And death.

And motherfucking goddamn bullshit.

2.

The first time I went upstairs and knocked on his door to ask him to stop, he didn't respond for a few minutes, he just lowered the volume on the videogame.

When I knocked some more, he opened his door a little.

He looked very small and scared and tired.

I said, "Are you uh, playing videogames loudly and yelling a lot."

He said no, but that yes, he had heard it and then he said he thought that sound was coming from across the hall.

When I told him I lived beneath him and could hear "like, stomping, and yelling too" he said no, but that yes, he had heard it, and man, he thought the sound was coming from my apartment.

I didn't say anything for a little bit, just maintained eye contact.

Then I said, "Oh. Alright, thanks."

Walked back downstairs.

3.

A couple days later, he was yelling and breaking things really early.

I went back upstairs.

It was weird trying to think of what to say.

Are you supposed to say, "Hey, me again."

Or "Remember me?"

I paused halfway up the stairs and thought of multiple scenarios.

Like—him answering the door and denying it again and me

nodding, saying, "Ok, but this is your last chance" then I turn and jump down the stairs to the next floor.

Or—him answering the door and denying it and then I ask him to help me find the apartment where the screaming and stomping were coming from and then we become best friends as we solve the mystery of who's playing videogames and stomping and yelling.

Him answering the door, me nodding upwards and saying, "Need a friend?" then walking into his apartment and picking up a videogame controller and being his friend.

Him answering the door and me just running back downstairs, tripping down the last three stairs and breaking my ankle then hitting my face against the wall.

Him answering the door, me smiling and pointing, saying, "Hey, just wondering if you could stop screaming at the videogame you're playing" and then he says, "Of course, my child" and disappears into a pale blue light and I walk into his apartment and play the videogame alone and someone knocks on the door and asks me to stop yelling and stomping.

It'd be great if he was just doing a puzzle and he came to the door, opened it, then casually said, "Yes? What is it, I'm doing a puzzle" gesturing into his apartment where there was a partly-constructed puzzle on the floor.

But it didn't matter because he just turned down the volume when I knocked, didn't answer the door.

4.

The last time I interacted with videogame guy upstairs was right before he moved out.

He was playing videogames loudly.

Yelling and stomping his feet.

From my room right below, I yelled, "Shut the fuck up."

He turned down the videogame and stopped yelling and stomping.

Made me want to yell, "Pay my rent too, and buy me a fucking hermit crab."

INSTA-FAMOUS: AUTUMN CHRISTIAN

I moved to California because I wanted to be an actress. It's too bad that I've got a face with cynical cheekbones and heroin chic died in the 90s. The casting directors say I have villainous eyes, and a smile that people despise, and I can never quite remember my lines. But, I've been practicing my enunciation. Susan sells sea shells by the seashore. Susan sells the sea shells by the— Fuck! It's time to face reality. The talent just isn't there. I could never play a leading lady in a romantic comedy or a sexy spy in a techno-thriller. I'm too awkward, too weird, too clumsy, too viscous, too murderous, too hyperbolic, too —me—

So what I needed to do was to get better at playing me. To construct an image of myself that'd be able to play me better than I ever could.

—That—was my path to immortality.

I certainly wasn't going to become famous on the big screen.

So instead, I created an Instagram account.

On Instagram, there were no gatekeepers in stiff suits, determining my fate with a tired sideways wave, no open casting calls, no standing in steaming rooms with five hundred other women, thinking—should I go on another juice fast? I think I forgot to wax, biting my nails down into new moons waiting for the phone to ring, maybe —this!— time, my dream will come true. No. Now all I have to do is point my phone at that carefully arranged cheese board at my favorite hipster food joint, click!, use the Gingham filter (The most popular), hashtag it, and publish. Simple.

Now, listen. I said it was simple, I didn't say it was easy. I didn't get

Insta-famous for nothing. Trying to take a shot of your adidas so that the right angle becomes a representation of a new ideology. You think it's just a picture of some new kicks on shiny white tile? Just another snap of a Starbucks pumpkin spice latte? You're wrong. This outfit of the day is the origin point of my eternal soul. I won't be just another vessel for someone else's fountainhead. I don't have to listen to anyone's ideas about how to move, to breathe, to think. I'm not a funnel to pipe through another's worldview, a prop to be positioned upon all the other useless objects in a little palace of perfect.

I'm an Instagram star. Now the world gets to be funneled through me.

My followers grew quickly. I had enough heart emojis to give Eros a run for his money. But instead of hearts my bows & arrows were slinging sponsored posts from Korean clothing brands. I've got sponsorships all the way from Dubai to Denmark. Haven't you heard? I'm hot like Chanel's little sister, like an inferno in an infernal internship. Boy photographers want to take me to Paris, to ride on yachts and pose with furs and fluted champagne next to their watermarks.

Was it really only yesterday that I was just a poor wannabe, eating soup of the can and hardly able to keep the lights on? Sitting outside of closed gates, begging for losers to notice me? Now people pay me to show up to their parties! I'm on the inside looking out, and my stacks are growing so fast that I can't even articulate how it seems like all at once I'm busting through boundaries that I once thought were as immobile as gravity.

I made it. I'm famous. Hashtag goals—Now everyone wants to be me.

Oh, I see the way you're all looking at me! Oh, this is just another morality tale about vapid millennials ruining the Internet with their Kylie Jenner obsessions and their vaporwave. You think it's just as simple as—Hold on—let me take a selfie! Please! I don't expect to be famous for nothing.

I said I wanted to be—me—

My vanity is a voracious art. I'm like a futurewave Frida Kahlo, except I've got LEDs in my flower crown and 300,000 likes for my eyebrows. I know all the variations of light that make my hair look like angel shine. Don't roll your eyes, this is renaissance shit. It's mythological. Better than biblical. My feed studies the phenomenology of unicorn frapuccinos. If you can't handle it, my 'gram might just blind you like the Tabernacle. @ my username three times, and I'll appear in your DMs like the devil.

Okay, I have to confess, something doesn't feel right. In the pursuit of glory I've just lost authenticity. My true artistry has been lost as metrics become my master. My sponsors are feeding me lines and I'm getting lost in between the spaces of their product placement. Act now, get a discount on this lipstick. Do I even wear burgundy? Scrolling through my feed. Food, friends, and fancy lingerie? It's all the fucking same. I have to admit, I'm getting sick of clean lines, pushing my laundry basket out of sight. But I can't seem to escape it. Even having a messy desk, and leaving Pringle crumbs on my pajamas is a statement. Oh, I heard quirky was a good brand! Anti-romanticism is really in this year!

I know that I'm better than all of this.

I'll tell you what the problem is. It's you. You people have all constrained my innate talent, my hunger to capture raw experience, devoid of all boundaries. You've choked my muse into complacency, crippled my expression with your mediocre expectation. I mean, how many more pictures of Ray Ban sunglasses do you need? How many more kawaii kittens have to be drawn in latte foam? Should I accept that it's fate, that the most popular pictures are of women in bikinis eating sushi on fake dates? Are you just afraid of someone who could be truly great!?

I wander the streets in a daze, phone out in front of me poised like a weapon, no trigger discipline, thumb waiting. For what? A moment of clarity. I'm a walking epiphany. Hashtag roadkill. Hashtag blood on my shoes. Hashtag I brought a knife to see if anything in this world is more than skin deep. You know I hate drama, but we've got to practice self care. 10% off on Lush bath bombs if you click the link, but there's no discount for this ticket to my dark night of the soul. Destination: a no man's land, a ghost-town. So buckle up and put your money down. You think I'm just another Internet girl photoblogging her breakdown? I bet you can't tell a Jackson Pollock from a preschooler's fingerpainting!

Hold on.

There's a new sensation in my bones coming up from the bottom of my being like a seismic vibration.

I can't see. I can't breathe.

Hashtag.... Where am I?

Maybe they're right. Maybe this is what a breakdown feels like. Yet how can something this monumental be mere mental illness? No. It's more than that. I can feel it. This isn't a breakdown, this is a break-through! I'm transcending my ordinary perception. This is a revolution, a representation of divine evanescence. I'm snapping pictures to create a new human expression. I'm capturing angles that might as well be transdimensional. The wounds I've inflicted open portals to new genres. No hashtag I devise can possibly comprise the magnificence of my genius! Oh, look at the gorgeous way the blood drips onto these autumn leaves.

Hold on. Let me take a selfie.

What do the comments say?

Creepy pictures! R U Okay?

U tryin' to be edgy now?

LOL! She used to be so pretty, before the scars.

Unfollow me, then! I don't need your approval! You'll be sorry that you won't be a witness to this great new moment in artistic history! You're all just microscopic specks waiting to be swallowed up in the ocean of the newest fad, whether it's dad bods, lip fillers, or overalls in plaid! Maybe human consciousness is a gift but I'd throw yours out with the trash! Washed up, uninspired, pathetic, sheep unworthy to even be ash that I burn on the path to the Internet Olympus!

Wait.

My numbers. They're growing?

It looks like even you people can't deny something this great! I need to to take another selfie.

Why is there blood in my teeth? Because I'm going to redefine what it means to be pretty!

Don't you turn away now! Look at me! Maybe you think I've lost it. Your comments suggest that despite your interest you're on the cusp of disgust and revulsion. Are you afraid of the revelations that I might pry from your mind if you stay too long to stare into mine? I have truly become the perfect representation of myself, free from the half-hearted restraints of lesser minds. Because I get it now. I'm not a freak, or a coward. I'm brilliant and you're lucky to be caught in the crosshairs of my prodigious dreams, each new scene that I create expanding the seams of aesthetic boundaries! I reveal to your eyes what you've tried to hide in half-moments of spontaneous relief, scrolling through Insta-gram searching for a brief distraction from your unfulfilling lives stuffed with overwhelming dissatisfaction. But no matter how many times you swipe through pictures of duck faces and new brides, you'll never escape the horror of being human, subject to the perversions of chaos and time. Only I recognize the truth you've tried to bury in-between Rolex close-ups and oversaturated lines. You live in perpetual amnesia separated from the source of your final biological destination!

But you don't have to remember, because I won't forget. I recognize this game.

I remember your face.

And I know your username, can't you see?

So listen, if I follow you:

You better fucking follow me.

ABOUT THE AUTHORS

Chris Antzoulis is a New York-based poet and comic book writer with an MFA in writing from Sarah Lawrence College. His poetry has appeared in *Yes Poetry*, *Newtown Literary*, *Luna Luna*, *FLAPPERHOUSE*, *decomP magazinE*, and others. He has also helped other writers reach audiences through his work with literary magazines such as *Madcap Review* and *Lumina*. He currently lives in Queens, NY, with his two evil cats and teaches creative writing at Mercy College in Dobbs Ferry, NY. For more information, or to contact Chris, you can visit chrisantzoulis.com

Lisa Marie Basile is the founding editor-in-chief and creative director of Luna Luna Magazine and community. She is the author of a few books of poetry, including a full-length collection, *Apocryphal*. Her book *Nympholepsy*, will be published by Inside the Castle in November 2018 and was a finalist in the 2017 Tarpaulin Sky Book Awards. She is also working on her first novella, to be released by Clash Books in 2019. Her first nonfiction book, *Light Magic for Dark Times*, will be published by Quarto Books in 2018. Lisa Marie's work has appeared in the New York Times, Narratively, Refinery 29, and more.

Maxwell Bauman is a halfway-decent Jewish boy from the Bronx. He is the Editor-in-Chief of *Door Is A Jar* literary magazine. Follow him on twitter at @maxwellbauman

Leza Cantoral is a Xicana writer & editor who lives on the internet. She is the Editor in Chief of CLASH Books & host of the Get Lit With Leza podcast where she talks to cool ass writers. Tragedy Queens: Stories Inspired by Lana Del Rey & Sylvia Plath is a CLASH Books anthology of stories that she edited as a result of being a Lana Del Rey & Sylvia Plath megafan. You can find her on YouTube at Trash Panda

Poetry & everywhere else as herself. She blogs at lezacantoral.com Twitter, IG, Facebook @lezacantoral

Autumn Christian is a fiction writer who lives in the dark woods with poisonous blue flowers in her backyard and a black deer skull on her wall. She is waiting for the day when she hits her head on the cabinet searching for the popcorn bowl and all consensus reality dissolves.She's been a freelance writer, a game designer, a cheese producer, a haunted house actor, and a video game tester. She considers Philip K. Dick, Ray Bradbury, Katie Jane Garside, the southern gothic, and dubstep, as main sources of inspiration.

B. Diehl is the author of the poetry collections *Zeller's Alley* and *Ballpoint Penitentiary*. His work has been published by *Hobart, BOAAT Press, Literary Orphans, Words Dance, Maudlin House, CLASH Media*, and other venues. He is also one of two editors of *Philosophical Idiot*. When he is not doing writing, editing, or breathing in dust at his warehouse job, he is usually hanging out with his cats.

Brian Alan Ellis is the author of three novellas, three short-story collections, a book of humorous non-fiction, and *Something to Do with Self-Hate,* a novel. His writing has appeared at *Juked, Hobart, Monkeybicycle, Electric Literature, Vol. 1 Brooklyn, Queen Mob's Tea House,* and *Funhouse*, among other places. He lives in Florida.

Gabino Iglesias is a writer, journalist, and book reviewer living in Austin, TX. He's the author of *Zero Saints, Hungry Darkness*, and *Gutmouth*. His reviews have appeared in Electric Literature, The Rumpus, 3AM Magazine, Marginalia, The Collagist, Heavy Feather Review, Crimespree, Out of the Gutter, Vol. 1 Brooklyn, HorrorTalk, Verbicide, and many other print and online venues.

Ashley Inguanta is a writer and artist who is driven by landscape, place, and intimacy. She is the author of *The Way Home* (Dancing Girl Press, 2013), *For the Woman Alone* (Ampersand Books, 2014), and *Bomb* (Ampersand Books, 2016). She is working on a new book of linked poetry, *The Flower*, which navigates how death changes us. She was recently accepted into the Sundress Academy for the Arts as a resident in Spring 2018.

Kat Giordano is a poet and massive crybaby in Pittsburgh, PA. Her poems have appeared in OCCULUM, Indigent Press, Rat's Ass Review, The Cincinnati Review, Up The Staircase Quarterly, and others. They have also been known to show up trembling on people's doorsteps in the middle of the night, too traumatized to explain what they've seen. She is a co-editor of Philosophical Idiot and can usually be found overindulging in her shoddy mental health at katgiordano.com or on Twitter at @giordkat

Justin Grimbol moves around a lot. He is the author of *Mud Season, Come Home We Love You Still, Hard Bodies, Drinking Until Morning, The Party Lords, Naked Friends, Minivan Poems, The Crud Masters,* and *The Creek.*

Joel Amat Güell (born Joel Amat Güell) is not an academy award winning writer, instead he just draws things for a a living. He has designed t-shirts and a huge range of apparel for a lot of clothing companies you've probably never heard of and for some others that you probably have. He was the illustrator of Horror Film Poems, has also illustrated comics, colored comics, and even read some comics. He has done other stuff too, which you can see in his website joelamatguell.com

Loren Kleinman is an American-born poet and writer with roots in New Jersey. Her writing explores the results of love and loss, and how both themes affect an individual's internal and external voice. She has a B.A. in English Literature from Drew University and an M.A. in Creative and Critical Writing from the University of Sussex (UK). Her poetry has appeared in literary journals such as Drunken Boat, The Moth, Domestic Cherry, Blue Lake Review, Columbia Journal, Stony Thursday Anthology (Arts Council Ireland) LEVURE LITTÉRAIRE, Nimrod, Wilderness House Literary Review, Narrative Northeast, Writer's Bloc, Journal of New Jersey Poets, Paterson Literary Review (PLR), Resurgence (UK), HerCircleEzine and Aesthetica Annual. She was the recipient of the Spire Press Poetry Prize (2003), was a 2000 and 2003 Pushcart Prize nominee, and was a 2004 Nimrod/Pablo Neruda Prize finalist for poetry.

Daniel Knauf created and served as Executive Producer of his Emmy Award-winning series, "CARNIVÁLE" (HBO). Mr. Knauf has since written episodes of "SUPERNATURAL" (The CW) and "FEAR ITSELF" (NBC). He has served as a Consulting Producer on "STAND OFF" (FOX) , "MY OWN WORST ENEMY" (NBC), the hit cult series, "SPARTACUS: BLOOD AND SAND" (Starz) and as show runner-EP on NBC's DRACULA and EP on the NBC hit-series, THE BLACKLIST. Additionally, he and his son, Charles Knauf, have collaborated on "THE INVINCIBLE IRON MAN" for Marvel Comics and the SyFy pilot/mini, "THE PHANTOM." Mr. Knauf has recently turned to screenwriting, developing a feature trilogy for Will Smith and Overbrook Productions, "THE LEGEND OF CAIN," as well as "A GOOD RUN." He has also been active in creating internet content since 1999, developing several award-winning websites.

Emily Paskevics, currently based in Montreal, is the author of a chapbook called *The Night That Was Animal, or Methods in the Art of Rogue Taxidermy* (Dancing Girl Press, 2014). Other publications include Hart House Review, Vallum Magazine, Acta Victoriana, Rogue Agent, OCCULUM, and UofT Magazine. She works with literary translation for OOMPH Press, and has contributed to Lola Who, Luna Luna Magazine, and Culture Trip. Follow along @epaskev

Christoph Paul is an award-winning humor author. He writes non-fiction, YA, Bizarro, horror, and poetry including: *The Passion of the Christoph, Great White House Volume 1 and Volume 2, Slasher Camp for Nerd Dorks*, and *Horror Film Poems*. He is the managing editor for CLASH Media and CLASH Books and edited the anthologies *Walk Hand in Hand Into Extinction: Stories Inspired by True Detective* and *This Book Ain't Nuttin to F*%k With: A Wu-Tang Tribute Anthology*.

Sam Pink's books include *Witch Piss, Rontel, Hurt Others, The No Hellos Diet*, and *Person*. His writing has been published widely in print and on the internet, and in other languages. He lives near Tampa, Florida, and sells paintings from instagram.com/sam_pink_art

Monique Quintana is the Senior Beauty and Wellness editor at *Luna Luna Magazine*, and her work has appeared in *Huizache, Bordersenses*, and *The Acentos Review*, among other publications. She is an alumna of the Community of Writers at Squaw Valley and the Sundress Academy of the Arts and has been nominated for Best of the Net. She blogs about Latinx literature at her site, Blood Moon and is a member of the Central Valley Women Writers of Color collective.

Sam Richard is the editor of the Weirdpunk Books anthology *Zombie Punks Fuck Off*, as well as co-editor (with MP Johnson) of *Hybrid Moments: A Literary Tribute to the Misfits* and *Blood for You: A Literary Tribute to GG Allin*. His writing has appeared in such varied publications as *NihilismRevisited's Strange Behaviors: An Anthology of Absolute Luridity*, *The Junk Merchants: A Literary Salute to William S. Burroughs*, *Dark Moon Digest*, *Splatterpunk Zine*, *Cvlt Nation*, and *Profane Existence*, among many others. He is available on any number of social media platforms.

Jayaprakash Satyamurthy is a writer and musician based in Bangalore, India. He has two chapbooks from Dunhams Manor Place, *Weird Tales Of A Bangalorean* and *A Volume Of Sleep*. His band Djinn And Miskatonic recently released its second album, *Even Gods Must Die*.

Danger Slater is the Wonderland Award winning author of *I Will Rot Without You*, *Puppet Skin*, and *He Digs A Hole*. You can find him Tweeting up a storm @Danger_Slater & at dangerslater.blogspot.com

Madeleine Swann's collection, *Fortune Box*, will be released by Eraserhead Press in June 2018. Her second novella, *4 Rooms In A Semi-Detached House*, was published by Strangehouse Books and her first, *Rainbows Suck*, was part of Eraserhead Press' New Bizarro Author series. Her short stories have appeared in various anthologies and podcasts including The Wicked Library and Deadman's Tome.She makes videos on her personal youtube channel and weirder videos on DADAkitten.

Joanna C. Valente is a human who lives in Brooklyn, New York. They are the author of *Sirs & Madams* (Aldrich Press, 2014), *The Gods Are Dead* (Deadly Chaps Press, 2015), *Marys of the Sea* (Operating System, 2017), *Sexting Ghosts* (Unknown Press, 2018), *Xenos* (Agape Editions, 2016), and is the editor of *A Shadow Map: Writing by Survivors of Sexual Assault* (CCM, 2017). They received their MFA in writing at Sarah Lawrence College. Joanna is the founder of Yes, Poetry and the managing editor for Civil Coping Mechanisms and Luna Luna Magazine. Some of their writing has appeared, or is forthcoming, in Brooklyn Magazine, Prelude, BUST, Spork Press, and elsewhere. Joanna also leads workshops at Brooklyn Poets. joannavalente.com / Twitter: @joannasaid / IG: joannacvalente

Stephanie Valente lives in Brooklyn, NY. She has published *Hotel Ghost* (Bottlecap Press, 2015) and *waiting for the end of the world* (Bottlecap Press, 2017) and has work included in Susan, TL;DR, and Cosmonauts Avenue. Sometimes, she feels human. Find her at: http://stephanievalente.com

Stephanie Wytovich is an American poet, novelist, and essayist. Her work has been showcased in numerous anthologies such as *Gutted: Beautiful Horror Stories, Shadows Over Main Street: An Anthology of Small-Town Lovecraftian Terror, Year's Best Hardcore Horror: Volume 2, The Best Horror of the Year: Volume 8*, as well as many others. Wytovich is the Poetry Editor for Raw Dog Screaming Press, an adjunct at Western Connecticut State University and Point Park University, and a mentor with Crystal Lake Publishing. She is a member of the Science Fiction Poetry Association, an active member of the Horror Writers Association, and a graduate of Seton Hill University's MFA program for Writing Popular Fiction. Her Bram Stoker Award-winning poetry collection, *Brothel*, earned a home with Raw Dog Screaming Press alongside *Hysteria: A Collection of Madness, Mourning Jewelry, An Exorcism of Angels*, and *Sheet Music to My Acoustic Nightmare*. Her debut novel, *The Eighth*, is published with Dark Regions Press.

WE PUT THE LIT IN LITEARY

CL◢SH

CLASHBOOKS.COM

YESCLASH.COM

ALSO BY CLASH BOOKS

TRAGEDY QUEENS: STORIES INSPIRED BY LANA DEL REY
& SYLVIA PLATH edited by Leza Cantoral

DARK MOONS RISING IN A STARLESS NIGHT by Mame
Bougouma Diene

IF YOU DIED TOMORROW I WOULD EAT YOUR CORPSE by
Wrath James White

THE ANARCHIST KOSHER COOKBOOK by Maxwell Bauman

HORROR FILM POEMS by Christoph Paul

THIS BOOK IS BROUGHT TO YOU BY MY STUDENT LOANS
by Megan Kaleita

GIRL LIKE A BOMB by Autumn Christian

PRACTICE MAKES PERFECT by Jayme Karales

HE HAS MANY NAMES by Drew Chial

SEQUELLAND by Jay Clayton-Joslin

THIS BOOK AIN'T NUTTIN TO FUCK WITH: A WU-TANG TRIBUTE ANTHOLOGY edited by Christoph Paul & Grant Wamack

THE VERY INEFFECTIVE HAUNTED HOUSE by Jeff Burk

WALK HAND IN HAND INTO EXTINCTION: STORIES INSPIRED BY TRUE DETECTIVE edited by Christoph Paul & Leza Cantoral